Exploring
the America
1803-1879

Produced by the
Division of Publications
National Park Service

U.S. Department of the Interior
Washington, D.C. 1982

National Park Handbooks, compact introductions to the great natural and historic places administered by the National Park Service, are designed to promote understanding and enjoyment of the parks. Each is intended to be informative reading and a useful guide before, during, and after a park visit. More than 100 titles are in print. This is Handbook 116. You may purchase the handbooks through the mail by writing to Superintendent of Documents, U.S. Government Printing Office, Washington, DC 20402.

About This Book
When Thomas Jefferson took office as the third President of the United States in 1801, much of the land between the Mississippi River and the Pacific Ocean was unknown territory belonging to France or Spain. By the time Rutherford B. Hayes left office as the nineteenth President in 1881, this land was not only part of the United States but it had been explored, surveyed, mapped, photographed, and was rapidly being settled. *Exploring the American West, 1803-1879,* is the story of how and why all of this came about. It is published in cooperation with the Jefferson National Expansion Memorial as one of a series of titles on major themes in the park's Museum of Westward Expansion at the Gateway Arch.

Library of Congress Cataloging in Publications Data
Exploring the American West, 1803-1879.
(National Park Handbook; 116)
Includes index.
    1. West (U.S.)—Description and travel—To 1848—Addresses, essays, lectures. 2. West (U.S.)—Description and travel—1848-1860—Addresses, essays, lectures. 3. West (U.S.)—Description and travel—1860-1880—Addresses, essays, lectures. 4. Explorers—West (U.S.)—Biography—Addresses, essays, lectures. 5. West (U.S.)—Discovery and exploration—Addresses, essays, lectures. 6. United States—Exploring expeditions—Addresses, essays, lectures. I. United States. National Park Service. Division of Publications. II. Series: Handbook (United States. National Park Service. Division of Publications); 116.
F592.E96   1982   917.8'042   82-12483

Part 1   **The Lure of the West 5**
                  by Richard A. Bartlett

Part 2   **Explorer, Mountain Man, and Scientist 17**
                  by William H. Goetzmann

                  Jeffersonian Pathfinders 21
                  The Mountain Man As Explorer 35
                  In Search of Exotic America:
                  European Explorers in the West 55
                  By Land and By Sea: Military
                  Exploration of the Great West 65
                  The Great Post-Civil War Surveys 83

Part 3   **The Pictorial Record 97**

                  The Artists 100
                  The Mapmakers 106
                  The Photographers 110
                  Index 126

Part 1

The Lure of the West

About the time that Americans were waging war with Mexico, talking of Manifest Destiny, and heading for Oregon and Utah, the New England author and naturalist Henry David Thoreau penned these words: "Eastward I go only by force; but westward I go free. . . . I should not lay so much stress on this fact, if I did not believe that something like this is the prevailing tendency of my countrymen. I must walk toward Oregon, and not toward Europe."

During those same years, George Catlin, the great painter of Indians, wrote that several of his New York traveling companions had considered themselves "West" when they reached Niagara Falls. But at Buffalo, Catlin conversed with passengers debarking from a newly arrived steamboat. "Where from?" he asked. "From the West," they replied. In Ohio he found farmers selling out and heading west. Cincinnati, he was told, had seen better days: it was "not far enough West." In St. Louis his boarding house companions were described as being "from the 'West'." Catlin eventually went "West" up the muddy Missouri to the mouth of the Yellowstone. He found the West a state of mind, as much a national leaning as a physical place.

After a trip to the United States, the British novelist Charles Dickens is said to have commented upon the unhappy pioneer who reached the Pacific Ocean and sobbed because he could go no further west. In the 19th century, Americans had a maxim that the first question Westerners at the Pearly Gates asked of St. Peter was, "Which way is west?"

Why the lure of the West? What is the attraction that draws people toward the setting sun? Perhaps the answer lies in discovering the simple motives of the early European settlers who began the trek when they trudged west from the forest-fringed shores of the Atlantic. So far as they could determine from descriptions given them by Indians or by traders and surveyors who had penetrated the wilderness, westward lay a temperate-zone Eden. Nearly 2,000 years had elapsed since Europe and the British Isles had been so wild and new. This new land to the west, so these pioneers were told, was covered with forests teeming with game useful for food and clothing. Occasionally trees gave way to fertile prairies of high grass. The land was drained by streams of clear, pure water abounding in edible fish. Here and there were great fresh water

7

lakes. Skies were filled with incredibly large flocks of birds.

To the newcomers, western America represented a challenge. As if by God's command, they wanted to bring it under the control of "civilized" people, raising the howling wilderness to the state of human society as they knew it. There was also the promise of new beginnings, of a life rich in all good things. The West only awaited men and women prepared to grasp the great opportunity before them. To this was added the mystery of what really lay out there, and the excitement and adventure involved in finding out.

Thus did the West lure the English and their colonists. By 1700 it was also attracting persecuted Germans from the war-ravaged Palatinate along the Rhine. As neighbors in the West, the Germans often found lonely settlers from Ulster, the land-hungry Scotch-Irish. Huguenots (French protestants) also settled here and there in the back country. Occasionally a colonial white aristocrat, with his slaves, headed west for new lands also, his eastern acres having become sterile from overuse. By 1776 these peoples were mingling in the valleys of the Appalachians and even forging westward into Kentucky.

The West attracted not just the ordinary family but also—albeit often as absentee landlords—men of wealth who wore powdered wigs and velvet breeches and shoes with silver buckles. To these affluent individuals the West represented potential wealth through trade and settlement. It was real estate to be sold. For over 100 years prior to 1800, eastern entrepreneurs had sent traders to fetch furs from the Indians, and surveyors to grasp the lay of the land for speculative investment. Most of these early land promotions failed, but in the process of developing their possessions the speculators inadvertently advertised the richness of the land, the abundance of the game, navigable rivers to carry produce to market, and the ease of getting there. Such information lured pioneers west in search of new homes.

Yet the progress west was slow. When President Thomas Jefferson delivered his first inaugural address in 1801, the new country still contained less than 5½ million people (not including Indians), and one-fifth of these were black slaves. The young United States still hugged the narrow tidewater region along the Atlantic coast. Seldom did settlement extend more than 50 miles inland, and two-thirds of the population resided there. The remaining third, the backwoodsmen or frontier people, lived somewhere beyond the Appalachians or hidden amidst mountain valleys. Here they remained, physically separated from the nearest settlements to the east by at least 100 miles of wilderness, until they felt the urge to move west again. Intrinsically, these "men of the western waters" seemed oriented toward the Mississippi River and beyond. As the 19th century got underway, it was clear to many that the westward movement would constitute a major part of that century's history.

Possessed as he was of a statesman's vision, Jefferson conceived of a West that stretched thousands of miles beyond the Mississippi to the Pacific. When he spoke of the Nation having "room enough for our descendants to the thousandth and ten thousandth generation," he envisioned American settlement of the entire vast area. Barring a few rivers and lakes to cross, and a region in the far northwest that he referred to as "the Highlands," where several major rivers were believed to originate, our third President saw no reason why the American people should not expand to the Pacific. Indeed, no one holding high office at the time was more fascinated with the West, and his insatiable curiosity led him to read all he could get his hands on concerning it, including books in Spanish and French. In Paris in the mid-1780s he tried to help a Connecticut yankee named John Ledyard, who proposed to cross Russia and Siberia, travel by boat across to North America, and then walk west to east until he reached white settlements. That project failed, but this did not deter Jefferson. Years later, back in America, he helped the French botanist André Michaux secure aid from the American Philosophical Society for a projected trip across the continent to the Pacific. Unfortunately, Michaux became embroiled in the unsavory schemes of Citizen Edmund Genêt, and his mission was cancelled.

Jefferson finally achieved success with Lewis and Clark, who started up the Missouri River in 1804 to explore the northern portion of the Louisiana Purchase. Later, he also sent men up the Ouchita and Red rivers in the Louisiana-Arkansas-Oklahoma-Texas region. Zebulon Pike searched for the Mississippi's ultimate source (which he did not find) and subsequently went west to the central Rockies. A lull

followed the War of 1812, but in 1820, during President Monroe's administration, Stephen H. Long explored Colorado from the Platte south to the Arkansas. In 1842 John Charles Frémont began his great explorations of the American West. His reports were widely read.

More information about the West came from private trappers and traders such as Jim Bridger and Jedediah Smith, artists such as George Catlin and Alfred Jacob Miller, and scientists such as geologist John S. Newberry and painter-naturalist John James Audubon. So alluring was the region that European sportsmen such as Sir William Drummond Stewart and Prince Maximilian of Wied came to hunt and see the wonderful new country. Fiction writers added still more interest. James Fenimore Cooper chose the West as the locale for his Leatherstocking Tales. Dozens of lesser, long-forgotten American writers in the period after 1830 also wrote on western themes.

Even as explorers, trappers, artists, and sportsmen explored the West, the plain, common people by the tens and hundreds of thousands were filling in what had been until recently the frontier. "Go West and grow up with the country" was the suggestion, and they heeded its challenge. For these people no sacrifice was too great, no temporary hardships too demeaning, to deter them in their westward drive. "There's a great day comin'," they assured one another. They were convinced that their new homes in the West would bring them a better life within the framework of a finer civilization than they had known "back east" or "back in the old country." In covered wagons and two-wheeled carts, leading pack-horses loaded with their worldly possessions, manning the "sweep" (the long oar) of a flatboat, the emigrants headed west. At times, it was said, the whole Nation seemed to have succumbed to the westward fever.

While thousands were making homes in the West, others were lured by the glitter of precious metals. California beckoned in 1849 and Pike's Peak—really Colorado's central Rockies—in 1859, and through the middle decades of the century many other regions were opened up to mining. With the intensive prospecting came stories of magnificent natural wonders: Yosemite, California's big trees, the Grand Canyon of the Colorado, the wonders of Yellowstone. One day people would come just to see these "beaut-

ies" of the country, even if they had no plans to remain there.

Before the Civil War, a dynamic booster named William Gilpin was busy ridiculing Stephen Long's judgment that the Great Plains was a "Great American Desert," insisting that the area could support a substantial population devoted to pastoral pursuits. With the war over and railroads pushing westward and a strong demand existing for beef in the growing cities of the East, the years of the open cattle industry began in 1866 and would continue until 1886. Profits of 25 percent on the investment were believed possible. Affluent Easterners, as well as British and European investors, were now lured west by the beef bonanza, while dime novel writers, always in search of new western subjects, made the cowboy a new folk hero.

In those same post-Civil War years, railroad promotions, the Homestead Act offering 160 acres of land free if it was improved for 5 years, new developments in agricultural machinery, and a series of wet years all lured new thousands of farmers into the Great Plains. The attraction was land, and with it came a new sense of dignity, freedom, and material well-being. Even after the West was settled and the frontier declared officially closed, there remained an afterglow of enthusiasm for western things, love of western vistas and western ways, right down to the present. Still, it is a certainty that the 19th century was America's century of the West. It has become a Golden Age, with tales of explorers and settlers, stage coaches and railroads, and cowboys and Indians, still gripping us in their timeless appeal.

These and other stories and themes of the westward movement are represented in the National Park Service's Museum of Westward Expansion under the Gateway Arch at Jefferson National Expansion Memorial in St. Louis, Mo. Of all the myriad facets of western American history, however, perhaps none is more interesting and alluring than the story of the exploration of the trans-Mississippi West between 1803 and 1879. It is this story which Pulitzer Prize-winning historian William H. Goetzmann synthesizes in the following pages.

Richard A. Bartlett

Part 2

Explorer, Mountain Man, and Scientist

The exploration of the trans-Mississippi West was America's greatest adventure and its most important contribution to a new age of discovery that dominated the 19th century. To most citizens of the western world, North America was an unknown country in 1800. When President Thomas Jefferson bought Louisiana from France in 1803, neither he nor Napoleon, nor the Spaniards who lived on its fringes, knew exactly what the United States had acquired. The width of the continent was known, thanks to Alexander MacKenzie's trek across Canada in 1793. Spanish and English mariners had charted the Pacific Coast with some accuracy. California was dotted with Spanish missions as far north as San Francisco Bay. Intrepid conquistadors and missionaries had penetrated deep into Arizona, New Mexico, Colorado, Utah, and Texas.

President Thomas Jefferson became the architect of U.S. westward expansion in 1804 by sending Meriwether Lewis and William Clark on their trailblazing "voyage of discovery" through parts of the Louisiana Territory to the Pacific Northwest. Pages 16-17: "Surveyor's Wagon in the Rockies" by Albert Bierstadt.

Coronado had crossed the Great Plains into Kansas as early as 1540. By 1800, however, only a few Spaniards had ventured out across those same Great Plains to the Mississippi in his footsteps. And to the north only a few daring French traders had ventured down from Canada to the upper Missouri that, for all one knew, coursed straight from the Pacific in a northwest passage. Jedediah Morse's map in the first American geography book (1797) was a typical summary of the white man's knowledge of the West: it contained mostly blank spaces or else mythical rivers and apocryphal kingdoms. Morse's map, like most others of the day, reflected a certain innocence and credulity. To most Americans, the trans-Mississippi West *was* a new world. At the great river America started over again.

Unknown to Americans in 1800, the country that stretched west beyond the Mississippi was so immense and varied that it stunned the imagination of those who eventually saw it, crossed it, came to terms with it, conquered it, or were conquered by it. First the Great Plains—a "great prairie ocean" some called them—stretched on forever, cut by innumerable shallow rivers along whose beds grew the only trees in sight. These rivers, principally the Missouri and the Platte, pointed the way across the otherwise trackless prairies and a sea of grass to the mountains that lay beyond. Early explorers called the region "The Great American Desert," and saw it as unfit for civilized settlement. Yet, in both summer and winter, it teemed with game of all kinds. Deer, elk, bear, wild turkeys, mountain sheep, badger, porcupine, rabbits, and wolves abounded; but the most spectacular wildlife were the vast herds of buffalo. To the first explorers the Great Plains must have seemed a paradise of flocks and herds, while the shallow rivers teemed with fish, beaver, and waterfowl.

Beyond the plains loomed the Rockies, foothills at first, then towering masses of craggy peaks, cut by passes and separated by "parks" or upland prairies. Great rivers—the Missouri, the Snake, the Green, the Colorado and the Yellowstone—tore through them, affording paths for the explorers. The mountains, too, abounded with game, but it was their rich, cold beaver streams that attracted the earliest pathfinders. Beyond the mountains stretched a real desert—the Great Basin—where a whole generation searched for that one river—the mythical "Rio Buenaventura"—that would provide easy access across to the Pacific. They never found it.

The southern Great Plains were more arid than the northern, and the southern Rockies were a formidable obstacle to travelers, but the old Spanish city of Santa Fe provided a welcome destination. Beyond Santa Fe was a country of terrifying grandeur that included the rugged valley of the San Juan River, the high plateaus of Utah, the gorges of the Little Colorado, and the Grand Canyon. Farther south there was little but desert and isolated volcanic mountain peaks. Beyond all these to the West, before one reached California, lay the Mojave Desert, Death Valley, hundreds of miles of sand dunes, 120-degree temperatures, and little water. After surmounting these obstacles, a traveler reached the southern Sierra, crossed over them, and, descending in stages to the coast, saw whales spouting out in the endless Pacific. The trans-Mississippi West was big country, so big it took a generation to even begin to assimilate it to the imagination.

It was not empty country. Clouds of Plains Indians—Sioux, Cheyenne, Arapaho, Pawnee, Osage, Comanche and Kiowa—followed the buffalo herds on horseback. The rivers were the homes of the more sedentary tribes—the Omaha, Arikara, Mandan, Otoe, and Kansa to name a few. In the mountains dwelt the Crow, Blackfeet, Gros Ventre, Flathead, Snake, Bannock, Ute, and Paiute. To the south Apache and Navajo waged continual war on the Pueblo whose stacked up apartment houses along the river valleys were among the largest man-made structures in the world. The Southwestern river tribes—the Papago, Pima, Mohave, Chemhuevi, and Yaqui—were ever present. Some lived in the forbidding reaches of the

Grand Canyon while others lived in wretched stick wick-iups out in the desert, subsisting on rodents, snakes, and insects. The Indians were as varied as the complex western landscape. To the explorers they were endlessly intriguing and exotic as well as often times dangerous and menacing.

The Indians were, of course, the first known explorers of the West. They knew the rivers and the passes through the Rockies and they knew the trails across the plains on either side. Nearly every exploring party depended upon the Indian's knowledge of the West, and the earliest explorers of the Rockies saw the logic of turning Indian themselves if they were to survive in the trackless wilderness.

Lewis and Clark gave peace medals to various Indian chiefs to help establish friendly relations with their tribes. These silver and copper medals bore the likeness of Washington or Jefferson on one side, and various inscriptions on the other. The one shown here is the Jefferson Peace and Friendship Medal of 1801.

Jeffersonian Pathfinders

Each age and each people produces its own explorers who, knowingly or not, traverse the same ground for different purposes and under different conditions. In the 19th century, the citizens of the United States of America began the great adventure anew. The first transcontinental expedition, led by the Great Captains, Meriwether Lewis and William Clark, will forever hold a place in the history of exploration. President Jefferson had planned and proposed the undertaking even before the purchase of Louisiana. In 1802 he had tried unsuccessfully to persuade the Spanish ambassador to grant the United States permission to send an expedition into the West (which Spain laid claim to) on a "literary" or scientific mission. Jefferson, nevertheless, was determined to go ahead with the expedition, and on February 23, 1803, Congress voted funds to support the project as a commercial venture.

In truth, Jefferson, ever a lover of science, had both objectives in mind. He was as interested as anyone in making contact with the western tribes and securing the potentially rich fur trade for the United States. But he also had much broader objectives. One of these was a lingering hope that Lewis and Clark would discover the fabled Northwest Passage across the continent. To this end he directed them to travel the Missouri and Columbia rivers in an effort to find "the most direct and practical water communication across the continent for purposes of commerce." If Americans could locate and somehow control such a riverine Northwest Passage, then the United States could dominate not only the western half

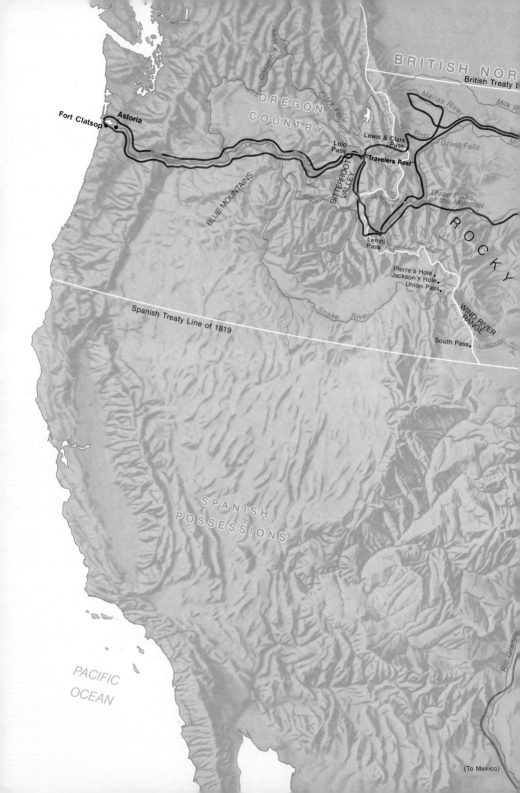

Jeffersonian Pathfinders
1804–1820

Lewis and Clark
1804–1805 (outbound)

Lewis and Clark
1806 (return)

Pike
1806–1807

Long
1820

ERICA

Site of Reunion
8/12/1806

Mandan
Villages

Arikara Villages

Grand River

UNORGANIZED

TERRITORY

DAKOTA
BADLANDS

Missouri River

G R E A T

North Platte River

South Platte River

P L A I N S

Sgt. Floyd's Gravesite

Pawnee Villages

Cantonment Missouri
(Fort Atkinson)

Platte River

Republican River

Pawnee Villages

MISSOURI
TERRITORY

"GREAT
AMERICAN
DESERT"

Kansas River

Smoky Hill R.

Osage
Villages

Arkansas River

St. Louis

Canadian River

Fort Smith

A R K A N S A S   T E R R I T O R Y

Red River

Spanish Treaty Line of 1819

MICHIGAN

TERRITORY

Mississippi River

ILLINOIS

Illinois River

KY.

Mississippi River

TENN.

MISS.

LOUISIANA

(From Mexico)

Meriwether Lewis (top) and William Clark. Their epic journey sparked an era of western exploration that lasted throughout most of the 19th century.

of the continent but the growing trade with China as well.

The key to such control, however, was knowledge of and good relations with the numerous Indian tribes who inhabited the region. Many a fur trader who had started from St. Louis and made his way up the Missouri had been stopped by the warlike Arikara or the Sioux. Thus Jefferson instructed Lewis and Clark to deal with the Indians very carefully and to study them in all their ways, whether war or peace. He wished precise knowledge about their customs. His love for ethnology would have demanded this in any case, but he also wanted to know in detail the structure of Indian alliances and their ways of making war and with whom. Beyond all this they were to report on the "soil and face of the country," taking due note of all animals, plants, and minerals that might redound to commercial advantage—or provide a base for future American settlers. In short, true to the scientific spirit of the American Philosophical Society for the Promotion of Useful Knowledge, of which he was a prominent member, Jefferson proposed to use science as a means of establishing a new farwestern frontier for America.

On May 14, 1804, the Corps of Discovery, as the 43-man expedition was called, left Camp Wood on the Wood River just below the confluence of the Mississippi and the Missouri near St. Louis. Lewis, who joined the expedition after the first two days, had been specially trained for the mission by the leading scientific men of Philadelphia. Clark, a bluff soldier, was the woodsman par excellence. Before the journey was over each officer had mastered the skills of the other and their remarkable cooperation made the success of the journey possible.

For 7 months the Corps of Discovery toiled up the winding Missouri, often hauling their heavy keelboat upstream by lines while rain turned the footing along the banks to mud. Along the way they had little trouble with Indians, and only one man fell a casualty: Sgt. Charles Floyd died of what was probably appendicitis and was buried on a bluff overlooking the river. Wherever they could, Lewis and Clark held councils with the Missouri River tribes in an effort to win their allegiance to the United States.

Winter quarters were established far upriver 4 miles below the Mandan Villages near present day Bismarck, N.D. Here Lewis and Clark hired fur trader Touissant Charbonneau to serve as cook and translator and who prevailed upon them to bring along his young Indian

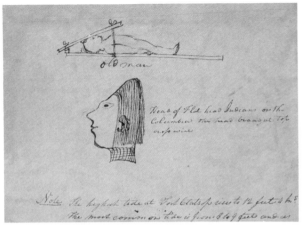

Few explorers have provided such exhaustive and accurate information as that collected by Lewis and Clark on the regions they traversed. Their journals and notebooks, laboriously maintained throughhout their journey, contain observations about the characteristics, inhabitants, and resources of the country through which they passed. As a result, they amassed far more reliable data on the West than had ever been acquired before.

These sample pages from their elkskin-bound journals give an idea of the kinds of information they brought back to Jefferson and, ultimately, the world.

Historians still debate the contributions of Sacagawea (above) to the Lewis and Clark Expedition, but she did help to smooth relations with a number of tribes along the way. Right: Reconstructed Fort Clatsop, Oregon, the expedition's 1805-6 winter quarters.

wife, Sacagawea, for possible assistance in translating. Here also they met agents of the Canadian Northwest Company of fur traders who inquired as to their intentions. Already a trading frontier or national sphere of influence had begun to be established.

In the spring a small party was sent downstream on the keelboat with scientific specimens and notebooks while the rest of the party continued up the Missouri. They traveled around the great bend of the Missouri, past the mouth of the Yellowstone and the Great Falls to the Three Forks of the Missouri. After some discussion they finally followed the western, or Jefferson, fork. Then, after crossing Lemhi Pass, they met Sacagawea's Snake Indian relatives, who guided them over the difficult mountain ranges of Idaho to the Salmon River and the Bitterroot Valley. From a point which they called "Travellers' Rest," near present-day Missoula, Mont., they crossed over, via Lolo Pass, to the Clearwater which flowed into the Snake and thence the Columbia. On December 5, 1805, they reached the shores of the Pacific. As if to document the presence of the United States on that remote coast, Clark carved on a tall yellow pine: "William Clark December 3rd 1805. By Land from the U. States in 1804 and 1805." Then they built the first American station in the region, Fort Clatsop, and went into winter quarters.

On the return trip the party divided after crossing Lolo Pass. Lewis continued over what is now called "Lewis and Clark Pass" and reached the Missouri above the Great Falls via the Sun River. He then explored the Marias River, during which time the expedition suffered its only hostile encounter with Indians. Clark generally retraced the outbound route, reached the Three Forks of the Missouri River, and crossed over to the Yellowstone, which he followed northeast to its juncture with the Missouri. There on August 12, 1806, he was reunited with Lewis, who had been wounded in a hunting accident the day before, and the Corps of Discovery proceeded down the Missouri to St. Louis where they were greeted with what fanfare the frontier settlement of St. Louis could muster.

The importance of the Lewis and Clark expedition was monumental. It revealed the geography of the Missouri River, the northern Rockies, and the lower Columbia to entrepreneurs and officials of the United States. It also inspired the public. And it established at Fort Clatsop a foothold on the Pacific Coast that would be useful in

Gateway to the West

From its modest beginning as a tiny trading post founded by French fur traders from New Orleans in 1764, St. Louis became the mercantile center and supply base for most of the western country, and for many decades it remained the chief emporium of the Louisiana Territory. Goods flowed through here into the Indian country and furs and peltries flowed back for shipment to Montreal, New Orleans, and Europe.

When the Louisiana Territory was transferred to the United States in 1804, St. Louis dominated western trading activities. Its strategic location on a flood-free bluff, convenient to the Ohio, Missouri, and other river approaches, made St. Louis the hub of mid-continental commerce, transportation, and culture, and a gateway to the wilderness beyond. It soon became the starting point for government-sponsored exploring expeditions like those of Lewis and Clark, Zebulon Pike, Stephen H. Long, and John C. Frémont, and for scientific, artistic, and literary travelers like Thomas Nuttall, John James Audubon, and Washington Irving.

Most of all, however, St. Louis was the headquarters of the western fur trade. Manuel Lisa, Auguste and Pierre Chouteau, William Ashley, William Sublette, and other leaders of the fur trade made their homes here and directed the activities of the trappers and traders on whom they depended. Along the waterfront, towering steamboats from the East and South met smaller river craft serving the frontier communities and outposts on the upper Mississippi and

Missouri rivers. Stores, warehouses, boatyards, saloons, and roominghouses were erected to handle the new business.

The St. Louis waterfront, shown here in an 1832 painting by French artist Leon Pomarade, remained the marketplace of the frontier for many years. Oregon pioneers and California gold seekers congregated here to buy tools and supplies before setting out across the plains. In turn, lumbermen, planters, farmers, fur traders, and local craftsmen sold their products to an eager and ever-growing clientele. Silversmith Antoine Dangen furnished the Indian trade with "well assorted Indian Silver Ware," including arm bands, head bands, brooches, hair ornaments, and silver-trimmed pipes and tomahawks. Gunsmiths Jacob and Samuel Hawken supplied pistols and a favorite rifle to trappers and hunters for more than three decades. Saddler Thornton Grimsley crafted dragoon saddles, harness, and military accoutrements for the U.S. Army. Sailmaker John Clemens kept a constant supply of "tarpauline, oil cloth, over clothes, dray and wagon covers, pilot cloth bags, and pack saddles, block tackles, splicing ropes of all kinds," to meet the needs of westward-bound travelers. And there were Newell & Sutton plows, Murphy wagons for the Santa Fe trade, and the castiron stoves of Filley and Bridge & Beach.

"It is doubtful," wrote fur-trade historian Hiram M. Chittenden, "if history affords the example of another city which has been the exclusive mart for so vast an extent of country."

Zebulon M. Pike led the first American exploring expedition across the central plains into Colorado and the Southwest. He discovered the peak which today bears his name.

later diplomatic maneuvering. Equally important, something of the richness and abundance of the trans-Mississippi West became clear, in official circles at least. Unfortunately, on the way to Washington, Meriwether Lewis died mysteriously on the Natchez Trace in Mississippi. The expedition's notebooks and maps were scattered, and the scientific collections were displayed as curiosities in Charles Willson Peale's museum at Philadelphia. The first published account of the heroic trek was Sgt. Patrick Gass' matter-of-fact journal, brought out by Matthew Carey of Philadelphia in 1807. It was not until 1814 that Nicholas Biddle and Paul Allen edited and published Lewis and Clark's own version of the expedition.

Throughout his presidency Jefferson's curiosity about the West continued unabated. He was, of course, particularly concerned about the boundaries of the Louisiana Purchase. He sent repeated expeditions up the Red River of Louisiana. One by William Dunbar and George Hunter in 1804 was thwarted by Osage Indians. Another led by Capt. Thomas Sparks in 1806 went nearly 700 miles upstream before it was turned back by a detachment of Spanish cavalry. Spain looked upon the Great Plains as a buffer between its North American possessions and the aggressive new nation. Questioning the legality of his purchase, the Spanish maintained that Jefferson had acquired nothing from Napoleon.

Ironically, it was left to the co-conspirator of Jefferson's political rival, Aaron Burr, to test Spain's intentions in the Southwest. Unwittingly, Jefferson had appointed Gen. James Wilkinson as governor of the Louisiana Territory in 1805. Wilkinson was in the pay of Spain, which sought to detach the trans-Appalachian country from the United States. He was also conspiring with Burr to carve out an independent southwestern empire at Spain's expense. But if he were to accomplish this he needed to know everything possible about Spanish strength in New Mexico and Texas. Accordingly, and on his own, he sent Lt. Zebulon Pike out across the prairies in the summer of 1806 with orders to locate the headwaters of the Red River, which was thought to be the northern boundary with New Spain. Pike's real mission was to reach Santa Fe and spy on the Spaniards.

Only partially aware of the devious machinations that undergirded his mission, Pike left Belle Fontaine near St. Louis and crossed the Great Plains, stopping to cement alliances with the Osage and the Pawnee. Far out on the plains he struck the trail of a man sent from Santa Fe to intercept him, Don Facundo Malgares, and followed it backwards towards Santa Fe. When he reached the Arkansas River, he sent his lieutenant (James Wilkinson's son) downriver with maps and dispatches for the general. Then he turned west toward the Rockies which he first sighted on November 15, 1806. He explored the southern Rockies for two months, discovered and named Pike's Peak, and climbed Cheyenne Peak from which he could see the whole of the southern Rockies.

Pike crossed the mountains and went into winter encampment on a tributary of the Upper Rio Grande, where he was taken into custody by Spanish soldiers. Knowing his mission was to reach Santa Fe, Pike nonetheless feigned surprise when captured by Spanish soldiers. "What! Is this not the Red River?" he exclaimed.

Stephen H. Long. Following his 1819 expedition to the Rocky Mountains, he called the Great Plains—now Kansas, Nebraska, Oklahoma, and eastern Colorado—inhospitable to settlement and compared them to African deserts.

Pike's capture by the Spaniards and subsequent release in Texas gave him the chance to reconnoiter practically all of New Spain, which he did with great acumen. Eventually he produced an extensive set of journal notes and one of the major maps of the whole West. Perhaps the most influential observation that Pike made, however, was his unfortunate characterization of the southwestern plains as a "Great American Desert" unfit for civilized inhabitants. This assessment—whether designed to camouflage the Burr-Wilkinson scheme or not—stamped an image of a desolate Southwest on the public mind for most of the 19th century.

Pike's description of the Great Plains as the "Great American Desert" was seemingly confirmed by Maj. Stephen H. Long's expedition of 1819-20. Originally sent by Secretary of War John C. Calhoun as part of a show of force on the Upper Missouri and the Yellowstone designed to frighten the British traders out of U.S. territory, Long's contingent was diverted out across the southwestern plains to the Rocky Mountains. A seasoned explorer and man of science, and accompanied by a corps of savants, Long surveyed the Great Plains and carefully mapped the whole region. He climbed Pike's Peak and measured its altitude, and his artist, Samuel Seymour, drew the first views of the Front Range of the Rockies. Then Long divided his forces, sending one part down the Arkansas River where several of the men deserted with all the maps and notes, while he continued in search of the sources of the Red River. Finally, so he thought, he found them and embarked downstream, his mission completed, only to find to his mortification that he had picked the wrong river. He had cruised down the Canadian, not the Red River. This was an important error because even as Long searched for that elusive river, John Quincy Adams was concluding the Transcontinental Boundary Treaty with Spain in which the exact location of the river figured importantly. Nonetheless, for the vast region he did cover, Long's work was important. His map of 1821 was among the most significant the country had produced in that it was based on the accurate fixing of geographical points. Unfortunately, his work was overshadowed by that of the more dramatic Zebulon Pike.

Three of Pike's concepts dominated American's thinking about the West for several generations. Most believed that the plains were a "Great American Desert" fit only for Indians and unsuitable for white settlement. Most also believed that the southern Rockies and the Upper Missouri country were close neighbors, ignoring the existence of what came to be Colorado. And finally a whole succession of explorers, geographers, and mapmakers agreed with Pike that somewhere in the heart of the Rockies must be "a grand reservoir of snows and fountains" from which rivers flowed towards all points of the compass. If the source could be found, then a navigable river flowing west to the Pacific was also certain to be found. The ancient Spanish myth of a "Rio Buenaventura" flowing west to the sea would not die.

Jefferson's interest in the West continued even after he left the presidency. With his strong encouragement John Jacob Astor, an enterprising New York fur merchant, launched what could only be called a global venture to the Northwest coast. Inspired by the Canadian Northwestern Fur Company, he formed the Pacific Fur Company in 1810 and the following year sent a party overland via the Missouri, the Snake, and the Columbia to the Pacific. Astor also sent a ship, the *Tonquin,* loaded with trade goods, around Cape Horn to rendezvous with the overland explorers at the mouth of the Columbia. His plan was to tap the fur trade of the Northwest and ship it to China aboard the *Tonquin.* This plan was perhaps too intricate and grandiose but it achieved several important results.

The overland expedition, led by Wilson Price Hunt, left St. Louis in March 1811, ascended the Missouri as far as the Arikara villages and, switching to horses, set out across the Dakotas in July. In so doing, Hunt and his men broke a new trail across the West. They negotiated the

Dakota Badlands, penetrated the northern Rockies, marched up the Wind River Valley, crossed the Continental Divide at Union Pass near the head of the Wind River Range, and trekked through Jackson's Hole, Pierre's Hole, and across the wastelands of southern Idaho to the Snake River, which they followed to the Columbia. The overland crossing, however, had not been an easy one. Game was scarce along the route; the Snake River proved not to be navigable; the morale of the party suffered; they became split and lost. In fact, not until the spring of 1812 did the final elements of the party reach the mouth of the Columbia. Hunt's expedition had discovered an overland route south of that taken by Lewis and Clark, but the country through which it passed seemed a mountainous desert rather than a western paradise.

John Jacob Astor. founder of the American Fur Company. His grandiose plans to monopolize western fur-trading activities ended when the British took possession of Fort Astoria at the beginning of the War of 1812.

While Hunt and his band struggled overland, the *Tonquin* and its crew reached the Columbia, entered it by passing over the difficult bar at its mouth, and in April 1811 set up Fort Astoria on the south bank. This represented still another claim to the Northwest Territory, though not, as it turned out, a permanent one. Leaving the fort in the hands of an acting resident agent, the *Tonquin* sailed north to trade with the exotic tribes of Vancouver Island. Here, in June 1811, trouble with the Indians developed due to the cruelty of the ship's captain, Jonathan Thorn. A tribe of Indians overwhelmed the ship and killed its entire crew save one. A mortally wounded seaman named Thomas Lewis managed to fire the powder magazine while marauders swarmed aboard and the explosion blew the *Tonquin* and several hundred Salish Indians to smithereens. Astoria's main link to the outside world was gone.

But Astoria was not destined to be isolated for long. The first contingent of Hunt's party arrived in February 1812 and by May trading activity had begun in earnest. The War of 1812, however, doomed the Astor enterprise. In the spring of 1813 John George McTavish led a ragged band of Northwest Company men up to the gates of the fort, informed its inhabitants of the war that existed between Britain and the United States, and demanded its surrender. McTavish and his men were soon backed up by the British man of war H.M.S. *Raccoon* but such force was not necessary. Astor's men quickly agreed to haul down the flag and sell out to the British. Some, like Donald McKenzie, even joined them. It was clear that Astor's objectives were economic rather

than political, and Jefferson himself was known to favor only the establishment of "sister republics" in the far west rather than an imperial extension of the United States.

Before Astoria surrendered, however, Astor employee Robert Stuart and six men (one of whom went insane) set out eastward across the mountains to St. Louis. Their march was full of hardships, and the possibility of starvation always confronted them. The Blue Mountains and the Snake River country proved especially difficult, and a detour far north to Jackson's Hole to avoid Indians nearly destroyed them. They finally arrived in St. Louis on April 30, 1813, having conquered the Rockies in the dead of winter. More importantly, with the exception of the detour to Jackson's Hole, they had located and traversed what would become the Oregon Trail. The most important features they had discovered were South Pass across the mountains at the south end of the Wind River Range and the Sweetwater River route to the Platte, which they followed across the plains. South Pass would become the "great gate" through which hundreds of thousands of immigrants would pour on their way west.

Two trappers indulge in an unusual moment of repose in this 1837 painting by Baltimore artist Alfred Jacob Miller.

The Mountain Man As Explorer

Meanwhile a new breed of western explorer had begun to appear on the scene—the mountain man. Part romantic adventurer and part self-made entrepreneur, the mountain man was a characteristically American figure who had no counterpart in Europe or anywhere else in the world. He was essentially a hunter who roamed the Rockies for years at a time, exploiting their bounty in beaver furs, enjoying the life of the great outdoors, while hoping to make his fortune. Some, like William Ashley, Robert Campbell, and William Sublette, did prosper, but most never quite realized their American dream.

The life of the mountain man, armed only with his Hawken rifle, a knife, maybe a hatchet, and a small "possibles sack" into which he stuffed food, tobacco, small tools, and bullets, was rugged and dangerous. If the perils of nature, starvations or wild animals did not get him, hostile Indians tried to. Nonetheless, the mountain man loved the grand freedom of the Rockies, the adventure, and the questing after the new. This was what made him an explorer. And his life, so close to the Indians, so attuned to their knowledge, so adapted to their ways, made him an expert explorer.

The first mountain men were members of Lewis and

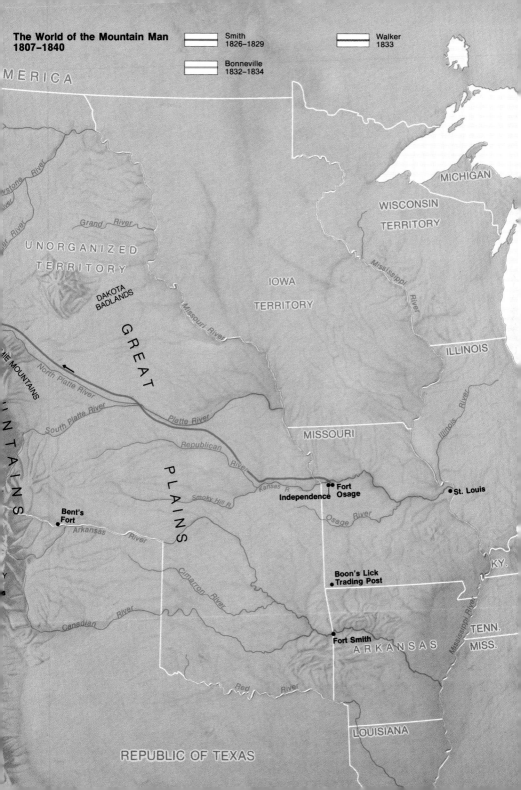

**The World of the Mountain Man
1807–1840**

Smith
1826–1829

Walker
1833

Bonneville
1832–1834

MERICA

MICHIGAN

WISCONSIN
TERRITORY

Yellowstone River

Grand River

UNORGANIZED
TERRITORY

DAKOTA
BADLANDS

Missouri River

IOWA
TERRITORY

Mississippi River

ILLINOIS

G R E A T

North Platte River

South Platte River

Platte River

Republican River

MISSOURI

Illinois River

ME MOUNTAINS

P L A I N S

Smoky Hill R.

Kansas R.

• • Fort
Osage
Independence

• St. Louis

Bent's
Fort

Arkansas River

Osage River

Cimarron River

Boon's Lick
• Trading Post

KY.

Canadian River

• Fort Smith

A R K A N S A S

Mississippi River

TENN.

MISS.

Red River

LOUISIANA

REPUBLIC OF TEXAS

Manuel Lisa. Many of his contemporaries considered him a scoundrel, but his trapping expeditions to the upper Missouri River and beyond spurred St. Louis' economic growth and added substantially to knowledge of the trans-Mississippi West.

Clark's Corps of Discovery. Pvt. John Colter left the expedition on the way home, far up the Missouri, to join two outward bound hunters for a season of beaver trapping. George Drouillard also became a famous mountain man shortly after. Both men worked for Manuel Lisa, a wily Spaniard who had come to St. Louis from New Orleans, and of whom it was said "rascality sat on every aspect of his dark-complexioned Mexican face." So hated by most of his men that he dare not turn his back on them, Lisa was nonetheless a very successful fur trade entrepreneur.

Lisa immediately grasped the potential of Lewis and Clark's discoveries. Forbidden by Federal authorities to operate in the new Louisiana Territory, as early as April 1807 he nonetheless launched a 42-man expedition up the Missouri. Making his way past the now-hostile river tribes, especially the Arikara, he established a fort (Manuel's Fort) in the heart of the Rocky Mountain Indian country at the junction of the Bighorn and Yellowstone rivers in central Montana. From there he sent out small parties of men in all directions. In the winter of 1807, John Colter, armed with only a pistol and a pack of trade goods, set off westward past present-day Cody, Wyo., where he discovered an extensive geyser basin forever after dubbed (in derision) "Colter's Hell." More importantly, he crossed over the Absaroka Mountains into the wintery beauty of Jackson's Hole, and thence past the towering Tetons to Pierre's Hole. After wintering here, Colter turned for home. On the way back he discovered the wonders of what is now Yellowstone Park. Few, however, would believe his stories about what he had seen.

While Colter was adventuring to the southwest in Pierre's Hole, George Drouillard explored the entire Tongue River and Big Horn Basins. He drew a crude map of where he had been, alluding to the supposed existence of Spanish outposts a "few days" march south on the Green River. He had looked for a transmontane passage southward to those Spanish settlements, but he could not get over the relatively low Owl Creek Range into the Wind River Valley, which would have led him to South Pass. From there he could have crossed westward to the Green River and the area of the supposed Spanish settlements. Nonetheless, Drouillard possessed great knowledge of the northern beaver country, which, because of his map, did not die with him when he was killed on John Colter's last expedition to the Three Forks of the Missouri in 1810.

Still another of Lisa's explorers did succeed, though with great hardship and difficulty, in breaking out to the south. In 1811 Ezekiel Williams and a band of trappers marched southeast of the Big Horn Mountains, crossed the valley of the North Platte and continued south, west of the front range of the Rockies, through the beautiful interior parks of Colorado. Unfortunately, most of his band were either killed or captured by the Arapaho. Williams himself was captured, but favored by luck, he was rescued after several months and sent on his way down the Arkansas River, arriving at Boon's Lick Trading Post in September 1813. Williams had discovered Colorado and its rich, beautiful beaver country beyond the mountains. His knowledge, which never reached cartographers, should have made clear the immense north-south distance of the Rocky Mountain country.

While Lisa's men were exploring the tributaries of the Upper Missouri and looking for a transmontane route to the Spanish settlements at Taos and Santa Fe, Jacques Clamorgan, Lisa's secret partner, circumvented government edicts against operating in the Louisiana Territory and in 1807 had made his way across the plains and into Santa Fe hard on the heels of Zebulon Pike's ill-fated expedition. There he awaited the arrival of Lisa's men from the north in vain.

During the next decade increasing numbers of American adventurers made their way from St. Louis across the Southwest and into the Spanish capital. Most were humiliated and ejected or imprisoned by the wary Spaniards. In 1821, however, on the heels of Mexico's declaration of independence from Spain, the trader William Becknell led a party into Santa Fe and realized a handsome profit. The people of the northern province now welcomed trade with the Americans, and the trade was so rich that Becknell hurried back to Missouri in January 1822 in time to return the same year with another caravan. In so doing he laid out the Santa Fe Trail over which thousands of freight wagons and soldiers would pass.

Almost from the beginning mountain men filtered into Santa Fe and Taos. In 1822 William Wolfskill trapped both the lower and upper Rio Grande. The following year he ascended the Rio Grande, crossed over the Continental Divide and explored the San Juan River country of northwestern New Mexico and southern Colorado. He brought back a fortune in furs, and by 1824 at least four other parties had rushed to the San Juan country in his footsteps. Though the Spaniards had long

He came from Pennsylvania, Virginia, Kentucky, Tennessee, and western New York. He lived in the Rocky Mountains and ate buffalo meat, deer, elk, antelope, and mountain goat. He made his own clothes or his Indian wife made them for him. He learned to set his own broken bones, to cauterize his own wounds, and to treat himself for all manner of disease and sickness. His only contact with "civilization" came once a year at the annual "rendezvous" where he sold his furs and bought the few necessities the mountains could not provide.

He was part of that reckless breed called the Mountain Man, the "free trapper," who lived what novelist Washington Irving called a "wild Robin Hood kind of life" and who contributed as much as any other group to the exploration of the West. "From the Mississippi to the mouth of the Colorado of the West, from the frozen regions of the North to the Gila in Mexico, the beaver hunter has set his traps in every creek and stream," wrote Capt. Frederick Ruxton of the Brit-

ish Army, who knew and admired them.

"They had," wrote another who knew them well, "little fear of God and none at all of the devil." Half-civilized, half-savage, with unkempt hair hanging to their shoulders, their faces burned dark from life in the open and obscured beneath beards, these buckskin-clad mountain men brought the western fur trade to its height in the 1820s and 1830s. And when the trade died in the 1840s, faded into the pages of history and legend.

Left: "Louis-Mountain Trapper," by Alfred Jacob Miller, 1837. In appearance there was little to distinguish the mountain man from the Indian.

During the heyday of the free trapper, about 100,000 beaver skins were consumed annually in the production of hats for men. Beginning in the 1830s, hatters used more and more silk in the manufacture of headgear and the demand for beaver fur declined, thus helping to save the animal from extinction.

Hawken pistol, one of several types favored by the mountain men.

The standard hand-made beaver trap, like the one shown here, remained essentially unchanged from 1750 through the 1850s.

ago preceded them in the person of Padre Sylvestre Valez de Escalante (who was looking for a route to the California missions), these were fresh discoveries for the Americans. They went by two routes. One took them from Taos through the San Luis Valley and along the Uncompagre and Gunnison rivers in western Colorado to the Green River as far as the Uinta Mountains. Another took them via the Chama, the San Juan, and the Dolores rivers to the Green, which teemed with beaver. One of these parties, led by a large rotund mountain man, Etienne Provost, circled around the Uinta Mountains and made its way down Weber River Canyon through the Wasatch Range and became some of the first Americans to see the Great Salt Lake. No Spaniard, not even Escalante, had stumbled upon it before American trappers coming up from the south and down from the north. The year of its discovery was 1825.

Other bands of southwestern trapper-explorers struck off to the west. In 1824 Sylvester Pattie and his son James Ohio Pattie trapped the Gila River. Then in 1826 the Patties joined a band led by Ewing Young that traveled west along the Gila, then north to the rim of the Grand Canyon. Largely ignoring this marvel, which they were the first Americans to see, they headed northeast via the Little Colorado to the Grand River (now the Colorado), which they followed to its source in the Colorado Rockies. Pattie's account of the journey asserts that they then marched north via the parks of Colorado to the Bighorn and the Yellowstone, but it seems more likely that Ewing Young and his men reached only as far north as the Wind River Valley and the Sweetwater before they returned to Santa Fe. At any rate, theirs had been among the most incredible western journeys to date, for they had traversed the West diagonally from the far southwest at the junction of the Gila and the Colorado to the northern ranges of the Rockies, linking up with the country Drouillard had explored in 1809-10. And along the way they had seen the Grand Canyon and the majestic country of the Colorado River Plateau.

The other achievement of the southwestern mountain men was the opening of a route from Santa Fe to the Pacific. In 1827 the Patties again followed the Gila, this time to the Colorado, the Colorado to its mouth in the Gulf of California, and then north across the desert. Guided by Yuma Indians, they reached Santa Catalina Mission in Baja California on March 3, 1828, nearly dead from thirst and starvation. Because they were in Spanish territory, they were taken to San Diego and clapped into prison, where Sylvester died, leaving James Ohio to tell the tale of their continental crossing. (Even at that they had been preceded in 1826 by Jedediah Smith and Richard Campbell who, independently, had crossed directly from the junction of the Gila and the Colorado to San Diego. But more about this later.) By 1829 a Mexican mule trader named Antonio Armijo had laid out still another version of "The Old Spanish Trail" to California, largely following Escalante's route north of the Grand Canyon and then coursing south to a site near present-day Las Vegas, Nev., and thence across the Mojave Desert, over Cajon Pass, and into Los Angeles. By 1832 at least three trails crossed the Great Southwest from Santa Fe to California.

Far to the northwest, Canadian fur traders also began the exploration of the interior. In the continental United States, Canadian exploration really began with the Falstaffian-size figure, Donald McKenzie, courageous, daring, and one of the real heroes of western exploration. After his return from Astoria, McKenzie was rebuffed by John Jacob Astor, who was still angry over what he considered the perfidy of McKenzie and Astor's Columbia partners in turning Astoria over to the British. McKenzie therefore sought employment with the Northwest Company. In 1816 he returned to Astoria, or Fort George as it was called under British occupation. At first, because of his physical appearance and his previous work for the opposition, he was not taken seriously; but in a year's time he revitalized all of the company's posts in the Northwest—primarily by constantly making friends with the Indians. Ever since his overland trek with the Astorians, however, McKenzie had been struck by the possibilities of the Snake River country. He saw that it led straight to the heart of the Rocky Mountains beaver country. Therefore, in 1818 he led the first of the Northwest Company's Snake River brigades to the junction of the Snake and the Columbia, where he built a trading fort. Then he set off across the Blue Mountains toward the Skamnaugh, or Boise, River in western Idaho. He continued east, trapping the tributaries of the Snake until he reached the country between the Snake and the Green rivers. He also trekked north to Jackson's Hole.

The next year, 1819, in experimenting with supplying his field parties by water, McKenzie became the first man to traverse Hell's Canyon of the Snake River. He led his men as far east as Bear Lake in eastern Utah but he

Canadian-born Peter Skene Ogden spent most of his adult life working for the Hudson's Bay Company. He was one of the first to explore the Great Salt Lake region. He was also the discoverer of the Humboldt River in northern Nevada. Ogden, Utah, is named in his honor.

never bothered to follow Bear River, which flows out of the lake into the Great Salt Lake; hence he never saw that great inland sea.

After McKenzie left the Northwest in 1821, he had several successors but only one could match him: Peter Skene Ogden. The son of a Revolutionary War loyalist, Ogden was known as a troublemaker and hellion in the Northwest Company. Aside from attempting to burn up a companion for the sport of it, he had also assaulted a Hudson's Bay official, nearly killing him, and he imprisoned a whole company outpost in what amounted to a mutiny in the wilderness. In 1824 Ogden, banished from the center of most Hudson's Bay Company activity, led his men southeast into the Bear River country, where in December they first glimpsed, without realizing what they were seeing, the Great Salt Lake. In the spring of 1825 Ogden and his Canadians made contact with American mountain men at Mountain Green, just east of the Great Salt Lake. Here most of his men deserted to the Americans, and Ogden made his way back to Fort Nez Perce only with difficulty.

Between 1825 and 1830 Ogden made five more trips into the western interior. He marched south into California via the Willamette Valley and opened up a new route to Mexican territory. He discovered the Humboldt River that flows across northern Nevada. (This became a vital link in the trail to California followed by American emigrants a decade later.) He explored the northern shores of the Great Salt Lake. And he made a remarkable journey south from the Humboldt Sinks in Nevada to the Colorado River near Needles, Calif., and thence to the mouth of the Colorado at the Gulf of California. He had crossed the Great Basin from north to south and, along with Jedediah Smith, was perhaps the only explorer of the era to traverse the entire West from north to south. By 1830 he knew more about the West beyond the Wasatch Mountains than any other man except Jedediah Smith. His knowledge was recorded on the latest French and British maps by A.H. Brue of Paris and Aaron Arrowsmith of London. This information thus became available to Americans and, ironically, helped to speed the demise of the British in the Northwest.

After the Astorians' abortive adventures and the daring forays of Lisa's parties, the major American inroads into the West were made by men of the Rocky Mountain Fur Company. In February 1822 Gen. William Ashley of St. Louis placed an advertisement in the St. Louis *Gazette* and *Public Advertiser* calling for "Enterprising Young Men . . . to ascend the Missouri to its source, there to be employed for one, two or three years." Ashley's call was answered by some who became the greatest of all mountain men-explorers: Jedediah Smith, Thomas Fitzpatrick, David Jackson, William Sublette, James Clyman, Edward Rose, Hugh Glass, Jim Bridger. Ashley himself was an adventuresome, imaginative man who had great flair—and ambition. A Virginian of aristocratic mien, he aspired to great and sudden wealth to finance a political career. This he hoped to achieve with the help of his seasoned partner Andrew Henry (one of Lisa's old engagees) and the "Enterprising Young Men."

At first Ashley's expeditions came to disaster. One of his large keelboats sank in the Missouri with all the trade goods aboard. A second expedition was pinned down and all but destroyed by the fierce Arikara on a sandbar in the river opposite their villages. Clearly with the Indians all along the Missouri aroused, there was no chance of moving in the wake of Lewis and Clark by 1824, so Ashley determined to take his parties overland. Andrew Henry led one band to the Yellowstone, eventually establishing a post at the confluence of the Yellowstone and Powder rivers. From there he sent John H. Weber and a band that included Jim Bridger across into the Wind River Valley to winter with friendly Crow Indians.

The other party was led by Jedediah Strong Smith, perhaps the greatest of all mountain men and one of America's greatest explorers. Smith was only 24 years old, but he had been struck with exploring fever ever since a family friend had given him a copy of Biddle and Allen's account of the Lewis and Clark expedition. Smith was also a religious man, which perhaps accounts for his great courage.

On that first expedition, Smith took his men out across the Dakota Badlands to a spur of the Rockies called the Black Hills (the present Laramie Mountains). At this point he was attacked by a grizzly bear who seized his whole head in its jaws and ripped off his scalp and one of his ears. His men killed the bear but they held out little hope for Smith. Under Smith's calm direction, however, they sewed his scalp and ear back on. Ten days later he was again ready to take to the trail, hardly a handsome specimen with a patched-on ear and a squinted, sewed-up eye, but nonetheless in one tough piece.

Soon they made the Powder River, crossed over the Big Horn Mountains via Granite Pass, and descended

Gen. William Ashley's 1822 newspaper appeal for "Enterprising Young Men" to join him in his fur-trading venture to the sources of the Missouri River attracted a host of famous trappers and mountain men. One of those who answered Ashley's call was Jim Bridger (above), fur-trader, frontiersman, and army scout.

45

into the Big Horn Basin. Though it was a beautiful spot, they did not tarry there but joined Weber's band in a bleak winter encampment with the Crows in the Wind River Valley. There, despite the cold, they joined the Indians in hunting the buffalo that were seeking shelter in the mountains. Together they killed over a thousand.

At the end of February, Smith and his men attempted to get out of the Wind River Valley via the upper end—the same Union Pass that had been used by the outward bound Astorians. Deep snows blocked their path, however, and they returned to the Crow village. There the Crows, using a deerskin and piles of sand for mountains, showed them a route around the southeastern end of the Wind River Mountains. So, still in bitter cold, they followed the Wind River to the Sweetwater. Blizzards engulfed them. The wind blew so hard they could not light a campfire. Game was scarce, and they almost starved, but somehow they turned the flank of the Wind River Mountains. In so doing, they crossed over the Continental Divide at the South Pass, rediscovering (for the first time westbound) that great emigrant gateway to the West. Ever afterwards South Pass was used by most overland parties.

On March 19 Smith and his men reached the Green River, called by the Indians the Seedskeedee. There they split up into beaver trapping parties. Smith followed the Green as far south as the Uinta Mountains (on the other side of which Etienne Provost and his men, all unbeknownst, were struggling toward the Wasatch Mountains and Great Salt Lake). That same season, Smith and his men made contact with a brigade of Northwest Company men under Alexander Ross on the Blackfoot Fork of the Snake.

Meanwhile, Weber and his men had followed Smith's trail out of the Wind River Valley and across South Pass to the Green River. From there they trekked north to Bear Lake and the Bear River. In the early spring of 1825 one of their number, Jim Bridger, on a bet sailed down Bear River in a bull boat and came out in the Great Salt Lake. He became its official discoverer. According to a member of the party, Robert Campbell, "He went to its margin and tasted the water, and on his return reported his discovery. The fact of the water being salt induced the belief that it was an arm of the Pacific Ocean . . ."

The year 1825 also saw mountain men-explorers from every corner of the West come together for a rendezvous on a fork of the Green River. They had criss-crossed the entire West and thus could exchange information as well as tall tales, trade goods, beaver pelts, and toasts in rotgut trader's whiskey. The rendezvous, established by Ashley as a way of supplying his trappers, became an annual event after 1825.

In 1826 Jedediah Smith became Ashley's field leader, and in the same year conducted one of the great exploring expeditions in the annals of the West. On August 22, Smith set out from the Great Salt Lake "for the purpose of exploring the country S.W. which was entirely unknown to me, and of which I could collect no satisfactory information from the Indians who inhabit this country on its N.E. borders." Smith's route took him southwest past the Utah Lake and the Sevier River, then down along what became the "Mormon Corridor" to the Virgin River (which he called Adams River) and through the wonders of present-day Zion National Park. When he reached the Colorado River far below the Grand Canyon, Smith instantly recognized it as the same Green River which he had left at last year's rendezvous. He took his men across the Colorado and into the villages of the grass-skirted Mohave Indians. From them he learned of an ancient Indian trading trail across the Mojave Desert. After his men had rested, Smith led them along this trail and into the Mexican settlement at San Gabriel (near Los Angeles). His was the first American party to cross the Southwest into California.

The only known authenticated portrait of Jedediah Strong Smith shows him incongruously dressed in the garb of an Eastern dandy. He led the first Americans overland into California in 1826.

After remaining for nearly 2 months in southern California, partly because of the hostility of the Mexican authorities, the intrepid Smith led his men north to the American River. Here they tried to cross over the Sierra to the east but were thwarted by heavy snows. Smith, however, was determined to explore the country between California and the Great Salt Lake in search of a short cut to the annual rendezvous. Like Ashley and others before him, he believed that there was a Rio Buenaventura and he hoped to find it. So, taking only two men with him, Smith went up the Stanislaus River into the towering Sierra. After eight grueling days they made their way over the mountains via Ebbetts Pass. Now came the most difficult part of the trek, across the arid wastes of the Great Basin. Before them stretched a thousand miles of alkalai desert, with little game, no friendly Indians to guide them, and no landmarks. Following a generally northeast route that parallels present-day Nevada highway 6 they passed by the future sites of Ham Springs and Ely, Nev. Then they turned north, but still the endless

The Rendezvous

The "big doin's" in the life of the mountain man was the "rendezvous," a great annual get-together of traders, trappers, and Indians for purposes of trade and revelry. Initiated in 1825 by William Ashley, St. Louis businessman and founder of the Rocky Mountain Fur Company, these great summer "fairs" at designated meeting places in the central Rockies, usually on a branch of the Green River, gave trappers the opportunity to trade their winter's harvest of beaver and other skins for traps, guns, ammunition, knives, tobacco, and liquor provided by St. Louis merchants or fur-company representatives.

Detailed contemporary descriptions of these rendezvous are few. One of the best is provided by Alfred Jacob Miller, the only artist to document these gatherings, in notes describing his painting of the 1837 rendezvous which appears here:

"This [the rendezvous near Green River, Oregon] was our ultima thule, our final destination. Here we rested for a month under the shadows of the great spurs of Wind River Mountains, encamping among 3000 Snake and other Indians who had all assembled at this place . . . to trade buffalo robes and peltries for dry goods, ammunition, tobacco, etc. It truly was an imposing sight. The white lodges of the Indians stretching out in vast perspective, the busy throng of savages on spirited horses moving in all directions, some of them dressed in barbaric magnificence.

"The first day is given up by established custom to a

species of Roman saturnalia. King alcohol is in great demand and attainable, although selling at that time here at $64 per gallon. It sets the poor Indian frantic, sometimes causing him to run amuck, when he is overpowered, knocked down and secured from mischief. Gambling, ball-playing, racing and other amusements are in the ascendant.

"On the second and succeeding days all this is changed. The American Fur Company's great tent is elevated and trading goes briskly forward.

Here the trapper gets his outfit and gangs of them depart under a 'bourgeois' for the beaver streams to trap that valuable animal. Here we saw all the notabilities, the great leaders, both Indian and pale-faces. . . .

"From this place also we made excursions to the charming lakes that form a chain through the upper portions of the mountains for the purpose of making sketches of the scenery."

The rendezvous system brought enormous profits to the traders who brought the merchandise to the gatherings. Ashley, for instance, took home with him in 1825 furs worth nearly $50,000; the next year he took enough to allow him to retire from the fur-trade and re-enter St. Louis politics. The system lasted until 1840. By then the demand for beaver pelts had declined so drastically that both the trade and the era of the mountain man were on the edge of extinction.

desert lay ahead. On June 25 one of the men gave out and had to be left behind. Smith and his remaining partner continued on. Three miles ahead they came to an isolated mountain and water. Smith rushed back to rescue his marooned comrade, then they all pushed on until, on June 27, they beheld the Great Salt Lake. Smith and his two companions had done what no white man, and probably no Indian, had ever done before. They had crossed over the towering Sierra and traversed the Great Basin from west to east. It should have been clear from their trek that no Rio Buenaventura or anything like it existed. Smith was laconic about the whole trip: "My arrival caused a considerable bustle in camp, for myself and party had been given up as lost."

As soon as he could, Smith and another band of trappers set out over the southwest corridor route to join the men he had left in California. This time, however, disaster dogged his footsteps. The Mohaves, who had been turned into enemies by a fight with another party of trappers, massacred 10 of his men. Smith and the rest were driven into the desert and only with the greatest difficulty reached California. There the authorities were distinctly hostile, and Smith went by ship to San Francisco Bay where he rejoined his men out of reach of Spanish soldiers. The trappers then turned north towards Oregon, trapping along the way and enjoying great success. But on the Umpqua River, the entire party was wiped out except for three men and Jedediah Smith himself, who was away from camp on a scouting expedition. Eventually they made their way north via the Willamette Valley to the Hudson's Bay Company post at Fort Vancouver, where they were well received.

After recuperating at Fort Vancouver, Smith went up the Columbia to the Hudson's Bay post at Fort Colvile near Kettle Falls. While with the British, Smith noted the rich possibilities for American settlement in the Willamette and Columbia river valleys. Upon his return he drafted a letter to the Secretary of War to this effect, signed by his partners David Jackson and William Sublette. This letter was published by Congress and gained national prominence. It helped to arouse the enthusiasm of Americans for emigration to Oregon.

Meanwhile, Smith was not through exploring. From Fort Colvile he journeyed all the way to the Canadian border. Then, joining his partner David Jackson at Flathead Lake, he moved south down the Bitterroot Valley into Pierre's Hole for the summer rendezvous. The following season he and his men passed through the Yellowstone National Park area and on to the Big Horn Basin. From there they crossed over into the Wind River Valley and then swung north to a winter encampment on the Powder River just east of the Big Horn Mountains. The following year (1830) Smith continued to explore the Upper Missouri region. Afterwards he went downriver and seemingly into retirement. But his curiosity would not let him rest. He had never traversed the Santa Fe Trail. In 1831, while bound for Santa Fe, he was killed by Comanches on the Cimarron River.

Without question Jedediah Smith was one of America's greatest explorers. He had traversed the West from the Upper Missouri to the deserts of the far Southwest. He knew the heart of the Rockies, the Great Plains, California and Oregon, the Columbia River, and the Great Basin (which he was the first white man to cross). He had pioneered in the rediscovery of the central route across the Rockies via South Pass, and he had personally informed the U.S. Government about the rich possibilities for settlement in Oregon and California. He even left behind a map, the so-called Frémont-Gibbs-Smith map. On a Frémont map of 1845, Dr. George Gibbs of Oregon, apparently using a manuscript map given him by Smith, sketched in all of Smith's vast geographical knowledge, including notes made by Smith. Moreover, Smith's knowledge in less detailed form even reached the aging Albert Gallatin in time for inclusion in his "Map of the Indian Tribes of North America," published by the American Antiquarian Society in 1836. Gallatin's ethnographic map, reinforced by Smith's data, became the standard such map of the country until virtually the Civil War.

There were, of course, many other mountain men-explorers. Some were important because they were trailblazers for the emigrants who moved West starting in 1832. One of these trailblazers was Joseph Reddeford Walker, who had exploring in his blood and came to know more of the West than any man save Jedediah Smith and Peter Skene Ogden. A tall, handsome fellow, Walker was a Tennessean who gravitated to the Missouri frontier by the time he was in his early twenties. By 1822 he had already made two trips to Santa Fe and subsequently aided an official U.S. Government survey party in laying out the Santa Fe Trail in 1826. He also helped found the outfitting center for the southwestern expeditions, Independence, Mo., and served as the sheriff of that rough, brawling town. His exploring days

began in 1831 when he met Capt. Benjamin Louis Eulalie De Bonneville at Fort Gibson in Oklahoma. Bonneville was ostensibly on leave from the U.S. Army to conduct a fur-trading expedition to the Rocky Mountains. It seems clear, however, that he was really reconnoitering the central Rockies for the government and searching for a route to California. Though he proved to be a poor fur trader, Bonneville, thanks to Walker's help, accomplished both objectives admirably.

In the spring of 1832, with Walker as his field lieutenant, Bonneville set out from Fort Osage for the mountains. He followed the now familiar path via the Platte, the Sweetwater, and South Pass to the Green River. Eventually he built a fur trading post on Ham's Fork of the Green, a very unlikely spot which he eventually abandoned for the Salmon River further north. At the Green River rendezvous of 1833 Bonneville organized a party under Walker to march around the north end of Great Salt Lake and cross westward to the Pacific. Walker and his men intentionally struck out for California through what was still Mexican territory as unofficial agents of the U.S. Government. They coursed westward from the Great Salt Lake across great stretches of desert to Humboldt River, which they followed southwestward to the Humboldt sinks at the base of the Sierra. Here, in a starving condition, they were forced to fight a pitched battle with Indians. Almost in desperation they struck out into the Sierra via a southern branch of what is now the East Walker River. They soon found themselves crossing the mountains over a kind of pass between the watersheds of the Merced and Tuolumne rivers. In the course of their struggles they became the first white men to view the misty falls and breathtaking chasms of the Yosemite. They also came upon the "Big Trees" (Sequoia) at the foot of Yosemite as they descended into California.

On Walker's return journey he traveled south in California. Aided by Indian guides, he located a pass around the southern end of the Sierra that was practical for wagons and emigrants. (This was Walker's Pass, for a long time the chief emigrant gateway into California.) Walker himself clearly realized what he had done and subsequently led wagon trains back over the route he had laid out. Maps based on Walker's work were published in Washington Irving's two classic works on the West, *Astoria* (1836) and *The Adventures of Captain Bonneville* (1837).

For the rest of his long life (1798-1876) Walker trekked

Capt. Benjamin Louis Eulalie de Bonneville (top) was not the dashing western cavalier that Washington Irving made him out to be, but his explorations in conjunction with veteran Tennessee trapper Joseph Reddeford Walker (above) furthered the cause of national expansion. Left: Yosemite Falls, discovered by Bonneville and Walker in 1833, as photographed by Eadweard Muybridge in 1872.

all over the West, making many trips back and forth to California. He also guided wagon trains and herded horses along the Old Spanish Trail from New Mexico to California. He twice guided Frémont and was present at the beginning of the Bear Flag Revolt that helped touch off the Mexican War in California. His dream, however, was to explore the Green River down its course through the Uintas and the high plateaus of Utah. He was never able to accomplish this feat, which 25 years later brought immortality to Maj. John Wesley Powell. Instead, in the 1860s, after an extraordinary series of adventures in central Arizona, Walker found gold. The town of Prescott grew on the site of his gold strike, and became the territorial capital of Arizona. Walker's career as explorer, army scout, horse trader, and rancher spanned the age from the mountain man to the prospector, and encompassed most of the activities of the frontier West. Above all, however, he was a trailblazer.

In a sense, the "trailblazer" title fits all of that courageous band of men who entered the Rockies in the first decades of the 19th century. They succeeded so well at opening up the country that by 1850 their day was at an end. As parties of would-be farmers, miners, railroaders, and storekeepers roamed along the trails blazed by the mountain men, the life of the solitary trapper became less and less feasible. There were other more exciting tasks to turn to, such as army scout, Indian agent, wagon train boss, rancher, and gold seeker. And Walker's career along with those of a notable collection of other fur hunters—Jim Bridger, Kit Carson and Tom Fitzpatrick to name but a few—illustrates that they did just that. But before the mountain man's era was over he had made an unforgettable place for himself in the annals of world exploration.

Prussian Prince Alexander Philip Maximilian (left center) at Fort Clark on the Missouri during the winter of 1833-34. From a painting by the Prince's artist, Karl Bodmer, who also appears in the picture wearing high hat and striped trousers.

In Search of Exotic America: European Explorers in the West

The adventures of the mountain men and the exploration of the plains and Rockies attracted world-wide attention. To Europeans, the American West was a wild and exotic country full of strange animals and strange people. Though mountain men and U.S. Government expeditions were exploring the region in practical terms, Europeans wished to fit it into a romantic horizon in the manner of the German scientist Alexander von Humboldt, who in South America had explored the Amazon and the Orinoco, penetrated the heart of the Andes and

John James Audubon, from a pencil sketch he drew of himself at Green Bank, England, September 1826. An exhibition of his bird drawings had recently opened at the Royal Institution of Liverpool and he was, he noted on the sketch, "Almost Happy!!"

climbed Mount Chimborazo, then believed to be the highest mountain in the world. And so in the middle of the 19th century dozens of European explorers came to see the American West with their own eyes, prepared to be dazzled with its wonders. Theirs was a different kind of exploration and theirs were different discoveries.

One of the first of these adventurers was Thomas Nuttall, an eccentric English botanist who traveled far up the Missouri with one of Manuel Lisa's expeditions. He made abundant scientific collections, much to the amusement of his fellow voyageurs and mountain men. Nuttall's efforts were incorporated into a major work, *Genera of North American Plants* (1818). He also explored the Arkansas Territory and traveled to Oregon with Nathaniel Wyeth, a Boston ice-dealer turned fur trader, who blazed the final emigrant trail to the Northwest. When he was not out in the West, Nuttall taught botany at Harvard, and became famous for three things: his garden of exotic western plants, his stories of western adventure, and his curious attic office accessible only by a rope ladder that he frequently drew up after himself so as not to be disturbed. Nuttall was only the first of a number of foreign-born explorer-naturalists who traveled up the Missouri, the most famous of whom was John James Audubon who made the trip from St. Louis to Fort Union in 1843. By then the river trip was rather tame, but the intrepid Audubon, inspired by a lavish reception given him in St. Louis, seemed to regain his youth and made the whole expedition seem an adventure as he collected specimens for his *Viviparous Quadrupeds of North America.*

The most widely traveled European explorer was Frederick Paul Wilhelm, Duke of Württemberg. Educated at the Stuttgart Gymnasium, Duke Paul was inspired by the work of Humboldt and wished to follow in his footsteps. By 1822 when he left on his first trip to America the duke was already an experienced geographer and naturalist, having traveled in the Near East, North Africa, and Russia. Moreover, he was a member of the most prestigious European scientific societies and knew the most recent works on the American West: before leaving on his voyage he had carefully studied the first two volumes of Dr. Edwin James's report on Maj. Stephen H. Long's expedition of 1819-21.

In all, the duke made seven excursions into the United States between 1822 and the time of his death in 1860. Five of these trips were expeditions into the West. The

Audubon's insatiable curiosity about wildlife resulted in hundreds of paintings of birds and animals which stand today as monuments to his great and unique talent. These pictures, taken from Audubon's The Birds of America *and* The Quadrupeds of North America, *represent a sampling of the wildlife he encountered and painted on his western travels.* Top to bottom: *Ruffed Grouse, Columbian Black-Tailed Deer, and American Badger.*

Harvard botanist Thomas Nuttall. The plant specimens he collected on trips along the Missouri, Arkansas, Red, and Columbia rivers formed the basis for the Harvard Botanical Gardens.

first took him a thousand miles up the Missouri before being turned back by fur trade agent Joshua Pilcher, who brought news of the Arikara battle with General Ashley's mountain men. The only published account of the Duke's travels—that of this first 1822 expedition—indicates that he was a careful observer of nature and a great admirer of the Indians. He accumulated extensive collections in natural history and Indian artifacts.

On his second trip to the West, in 1829, the duke again journeyed far up the Missouri and lived among the Sioux, the Blackfeet, and the Assiniboin. He reached the Yellowstone and the Three Forks of the Missouri and managed to get himself rescued from the Blackfeet by the Sioux Indians. One of these Sioux he brought back to his castle in Germany, hoping to "civilize" him. Instead, during a sporting contest at arms, the Sioux attempted to brain him with a tomahawk. The Indian was soon afterwards returned to his native hunting grounds. Pompey, the son of Sacagawea of the Lewis and Clark expedition, whom he also took to Europe with him, had a much happier experience.

For most of the 1830s and 40s the duke turned his attention to Egypt, the Upper Nile, and other parts of the world. But in 1849 he returned to the West for an extended trip. He visited Texas, especially the settlements at New Braunfels, then moved on to Sutter's Mill and the gold rush sites in California, and, of course, the Rockies. He almost lost his life on the wintry plains of Kansas after being captured by hostile Indians, but he and his artist companion, Heinrich Bauldwin Möllhausen, ultimately were rescued by some friendly Otoes. The duke's 1849 excursion lasted until July 1856, during which he visited most of South America as well. His last trip to the West was in 1857 on the way around the world via Australia, the South Pacific, China, and the Middle East. By the time the duke returned to his castle at Bad Mergentheim, he was penniless. He had, however, assembled one of the finest ethnography and natural history collections in the world, of which his specimens from the American West formed a major part. Upon the duke's death shortly after his return, his collections had to be sold to pay his debts. Only the castle and a few paintings remain at Bad Mergentheim to memorialize his Humboldtean dream of a cosmos of knowledge.

The duke's artist, Heinrich Möllhausen, went on to a valuable career of his own. In 1853 he accompanied Lt. Amiel Weeks Whipple's army expedition in search of a railroad route to the Pacific. Then in 1857 he accompanied Lt. Joseph Christmas Ives's expedition up the Colorado and into the Grand Canyon. He was among the first white men ever to set foot on the floor of Grand Canyon and supplied strange, surrealistic drawings for both expedition reports. He also published his own accounts of the trips. Beyond that, he became one of the most famous and prolific writers in 19th-century Germany. Most of his 45 novels and 80 short stories deal in authentic terms with the American West. Though his works are largely unread today, "der alte Trapper," as he was known in Germany, was a famous literary figure, and through his paintings and his writings helped to make the Far West of the plains and Rockies real frontiers to would-be German immigrants.

At least one other German explorer of the early West must be recognized. In 1833, Prince Maximilian of Wied Neuwied, not to be outdone by Duke Paul, traveled far up the Missouri to Fort McKenzie in the heart of the Blackfeet country. He arrived just in time to witness a pitched battle between the fierce Blackfeet and the Assiniboin just outside the stockaded walls of the fort. Prince Maximilian, too, was a renowned and careful scientist. His collections, which have survived, indicate this. But he is perhaps best known for the spectacular work of his artist, Karl Bodmer, whose drawings of Indian life—particularly the soon-to-be-extinct Mandans—are perhaps the best ethnographic drawings ever done in America. His portraits of Indians, such as "The Big Soldier" in full regalia, are rivaled only by the drawings of George Catlin. While the prince was collecting scientific specimens and mountain men and soldiers were seeking paths through the West, men like Bodmer and Catlin were discovering the fast vanishing world of the Indian.

The British were not to be outdone. Sir George Gore hunted the Yellowstone. Capt. Frederick Ruxton emerged from Mexico and tramped all over the West with the mountain men. His classic work, *Life in the Far West* (1849), told the story of real trappers under the fictionalized names of Killbuck and La Bonte in such a way as to rival Washington Irving's *Astoria* and *Bonneville* for both English and American readers.

By far the most flamboyant European explorer of the American West was a Scottish baronet, Sir William Drummond Stewart of Murthly Castle, which stood on the Tay between Shakespeare's Birnam Wood and Dunsinane Peak. Because he was the second son of his family

Two specimens from Nuttall's collections: Flowering Dogwood (top), found near the Columbia River, and Crab Apple. From F. A. Michaux's North American Sylva.

German naturalist Frederick Paul Wilhelm, Duke of Württemberg, was an inveterate traveler. A member of the Royal Leopold Academy of Vienna, the Société Imperiale Zoologique d'Acclimation of Paris, the Society of Natural Science of Athens, and the academies of London and Petersburg, he had traveled widely in the Near East, Algeria, Russia, and the Caribbean before sailing for America in 1822.

From 1822 to 1824 Duke Paul journeyed up the Mississippi and its tributaries, including the Red River, the Yazoo, and the Ohio. From St. Louis he traveled west to the Platte and the Kansas rivers, then up the Missouri into fur-trade country. During his travels he gathered an extensive collection of plants, animals, and Indian artifacts, which he carefully identified and classified and took with him back to Germany. Additional specimens were added to the collection when he returned to the West in 1821-31, 1849-56, and 1857-58.

At the time of his death, Duke Paul had seen more of the American West than any other foreign traveler and had amassed the largest private collection of Western artifacts and natural history in the world. Some of the items from the collection are shown here.

Potawatamie headdress

Blackfoot scalping knife and sheath

Passenger pigeon

Black hawk

Top: *Sir William Drummond Stewart's caravan enroute to the Rocky Mountains in 1837. From a watercolor by Alfred Jacob Miller, who accompanied Stewart and whose field sketches provide a remarkable record of early wagon-train travel across the plains.* Center: *Fort Union Trading Post on the Upper Missouri. From a painting by Karl Bodmer, who visited the recently completed fort with his patron, Prince Maximilian, in 1833.* Bottom: *View of the interior of Fort William, the first Fort Laramie, in 1837 by Alfred Jacob Miller, whose paintings are the only known views of this important fur post on the Laramie River. For an exterior view of the fort, see page 102.*

line, Stewart could look forward to no great inheritance, and so he became a soldier, wanderer, and sportsman. He served with Wellington in the Peninsula Campaign and at Waterloo. In 1833, after an unfortunate marriage to a servant girl, he came to America where he intended to spend the rest of his life hunting and roaming in the wild West with the mountain men. In all he spent seven seasons in the West and saw most of its wonders. His first trip out (over what was to become the Oregon Trail) was to the Green River rendezvous in the company of William Sublette. From the beginning Stewart loved every moment of it—the sky high mountains, the gaudily painted Indians, the nubile squaws, the trading, the tall tales, the legendary trappers, and, most of all, the thrilling chase over the rolling prairie on horseback after the buffalo. From that first moment nothing in the world could match the wild free life out on the Green River. Stewart had discovered a landscape and a lifestyle.

From 1833 to 1838, Stewart traveled north into the Big Horn and Yellowstone River country; trekked south along the front range of the Rockies to spend a winter of revelry in Taos; traversed the beautiful interior parks of Colorado and made his way over the Oregon Trail to Fort Vancouver; spent a season high atop the Wind River Mountains; and gazed awestruck at the sublime beauty of Jackson's Hole. Finally, on one last expedition in 1843, he stood amid the wonders of the Yellowstone geyser basins. He explored and experienced the Rocky Mountain West during a period of momentous transition. Despite the high spirits at the several annual rendezvous he attended he could see that the fur trade was in decline. (In fact, he made an American fortune by speculating in New Orleans cotton himself.) He also saw the gradual growth of traffic on the Oregon Trail, beginning with missionaries like Jason Lee, Marcus Whitman, and Henry Spaulding, continuing with entrepreneurs like Nathaniel Wyeth, and culminating with a horde of emigrants who went west in the 1840s.

By 1836, wanting to record some of his wilderness experiences on paper, he began writing two novels— *Altowan* and *Edward Warren*—which were thinly disguised accounts of his romantic adventures with the mountain men and Indian girls. He also discovered in New Orleans a young Baltimore painter, Alfred Jacob Miller. Miller went west with Stewart in 1837 and captured in countless sketches, watercolors, and washes the rich sights of Rocky Mountain life. He recorded wild

hunts, escapes from Indians, trappers at work and at leisure. He caught on canvas the rendezvous in all its gaudy splendor, and he stood like some early Gauguin recording naked Indian girls at bath in a cool mountain stream. The butchering of the buffalo, the yell of triumph, the sight of panic and stampede, all of these he painted with a romantic freshness that somehow represented discovery as it impressed itself upon the imagination of his patron, Sir William Drummond Stewart. It was a kind of exploration that neither Miller nor Stewart would ever forget—even after Sir William returned to Murthly Castle to assume the duties of a baronetcy upon the death of his brother. Few men saw and remembered more of the West than Stewart, and none, save Bodmer, had recorded its swirling, pristine life so well as Alfred Jacob Miller.

In this fanciful mid-19th century engraving, John C. Frémont plants the American flag atop what he believed to be the highest peak in the Rockies. As progenitor and romantic symbol of professional exploration of the West during the 19th century, Frémont became the rallying point for supporters of the doctrine of Manifest Destiny.

By Land and By Sea: Military Exploration of the Great West

The West had clearly changed by the time Stewart made his last hunt in 1843. For one thing, a new kind of explorer had appeared. This was the military explorer of the U.S. Corps of Topographical Engineers. Officially formed in 1838, the Topographical Corps was composed largely of the best of the West Point graduates who were specially trained in scientific skills, engineering, mapmaking and topographical drawing. Though they worked on coastal fortifications, river surveys, and the mapping of the Great Lakes, in the 1840s and 50s they turned their attention to the West and became its dominant explorers. Their exemplar, however, was not a West Point graduate. He was John C. Frémont, a product of the U.S. Coast Survey, a protegé of Jean N. Nicollet and Ferdinand Hassler of that bureau, and the son-in-law of Thomas Hart Benton, the powerful expansionist senator from Missouri. In 1842 Lieutenant Frémont of the U.S. Corps of Topographical Engineers led an expedition to South Pass, the Green River, and the Wind River range to map the whole area scientifically. And though, like the Scottish baronet, Frémont was enough of a romantic to climb what he thought was the highest peak in the Wind Rivers and unfurl the eagle flag of Manifest Destiny, he was also reducing exploration (and public relations) to a science. For the next two decades Frémont and others like him from the Corps of Topographical Engineers brought the hand of government and the skills of science to the exploration of the West. In so doing, they were agents of

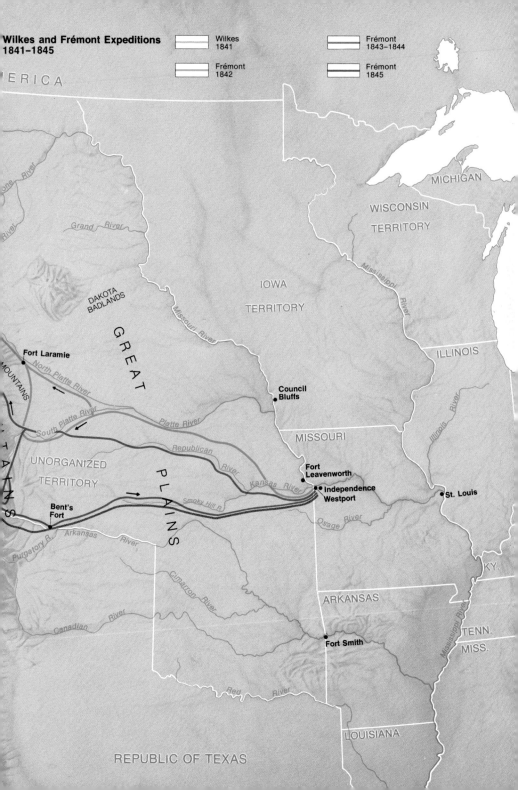

Wilkes and Frémont Expeditions
1841–1845

Wilkes
1841

Frémont
1842

Frémont
1843–1844

Frémont
1845

ERICA

MICHIGAN

WISCONSIN
TERRITORY

Mississippi River

Grand River

DAKOTA
BADLANDS

G R E A T

IOWA
TERRITORY

ILLINOIS

Illinois River

Missouri River

Fort Laramie

North Platte River

MOUNTAINS

South Platte River

Platte River

Council
Bluffs

MISSOURI

Republican River

Kansas River

Fort
Leavenworth

St. Louis

UNORGANIZED
TERRITORY

P L A I N S

Smoky Hill R.

Independence
Westport

Bent's
Fort

Purgatory R.

Arkansas River

Osage River

KY.

Cimarron River

ARKANSAS

Canadian River

Fort Smith

Mississippi River

TENN.

MISS.

Red River

LOUISIANA

REPUBLIC OF TEXAS

Capt. Charles Wilkes, leader of the 1838-42 United States Exploring Expedition to Antarctica, the islands of the Pacific, and America's northwest coast. The Royal Geographical Society of London later honored him for his voyages, but the U.S. Navy court-martialed him for mistreating his crew.

Manifest Destiny and servants of a rapidly-growing America whose citizens echoed the cry, "Westward the course of empire takes its way."

Going West in the early 1840s usually meant going to Oregon, which had become a focus of American aspirations. Frémont's mission in 1842 was to map the South Pass, a key point on the Oregon Trail. But even as he was carrying out that assignment, another expedition had returned to Washington with a report on the Oregon country. Capt. Charles Wilkes of the United States Exploring Expedition, a naval enterprise, had made a thorough investigation of the Oregon country as part of his great global exploring expedition of the Pacific Ocean. What he had to say about Oregon was important, but he was having trouble getting Congress's attention because of a flurry of courts-martial charges preferred against him upon his return from his world-circling voyage.

Wilkes had departed from Hampton Roads, Va., on August 18, 1838, as commander of a flotilla of six ships bound for the Pacific Ocean. His expedition represented a concession to the eastern seaboard maritime interests who were concerned about the whaling and sealing industry and trade with the nations and peoples of the western Pacific. In one of the epic events of 19th-century exploration, Wilkes took his fleet through the South Atlantic, and around Cape Horn to Australia and the South Pacific islands. Turning south, he coasted the icy shores of the Antarctic for 1,500 miles (in the process proving that the Antarctic was a continent), then sailed north via the Pacific islands to the Oregon coast. Here he divided his forces. Wilkes led one group of ships in an exploration of Vancouver Island, the Straits of Juan de Fuca, and Puget Sound. He also examined Gray's Harbour at the base of the Olympic Peninsula while searching for a viable port on the Pacific. The captain and his men found the beautiful coastline every bit as exotic as the South Pacific. It was a land of furcaped Indians who danced in hideous masks, sailed their carved 50-foot-long war canoes far out into the ocean, and studded their villages with mysterious totem poles that harkened back in some ways to the pre-Christian villages of the barbarians in the Danube Valley. Wilkes's scientists and ethnographers found the Northwest Coast a rich and exotic region for study.

The captain, however, was primarily interested in global policy and safe harbors on the Pacific shores, which is why he carefully searched the entire coast north

Illustrations from Wilkes' Narrative of the United States Exploring Expedition, *1838-42:* Top: *U.S. Sloop* Vincennes, *at anchor in Disappointment Bay, Antarctica, served as Wilkes' flagship throughout his voyages.* Center: *Members of the expedition measure one of the trees in the "primeval forest of pines" behind Astoria on the Columbia River. The tree's girth exceeded 39 feet.* Bottom: *Astoria, showing the encampment of Capt. W. L. Hudson's crew following the wreck of his flagship* Peacock *at the mouth of the Columbia in July 1841.*

of the Columbia. He also sent exploring parties inland: one from Puget Sound south to the Columbia; one up the Columbia past the Dalles, or rapids, to the Hudson's Bay post at Fort Colvile near the junction of the Snake and the Columbia; and one south through the Willamette Valley to California's San Francisco Bay. The latter expedition determined that there were no good harbors south of the Columbia and no large rivers flowing from the interior.

Meanwhile, Capt. William L. Hudson, in charge of the other half of Wilkes's fleet, came to grief off the mouth of the Columbia. He lost his flagship *Peacock* to the treacherous currents and sand bars at the mouth of the river. It thus became clear to both Hudson and Wilkes that the Columbia estuary was not a safe harbor. The only such harbors lay far north of the Columbia in or around Puget Sound. Thus Wilkes thought American diplomatic efforts should be aimed at securing territory at least that far north. But he returned home under such a cloud of acrimony over the methods he used to discipline his seamen that Congress authorized only 100 copies of his report to be published, and a lengthy court debate ensued as to whether Wilkes and Hudson were covering up for bad seamanship when they described the mouth of the Columbia as an unsuitable port. Neither Presidents John Tyler nor James Polk paid much attention to the valuable information he gave them. Perhaps the outstanding positive result of his expedition was that his extensive scientific collections eventually came to form the nucleus of the Smithsonian Institution after it was created in 1846.

Senator Thomas Hart Benton of Missouri was not unmindful of Wilkes's information, however, and on what he always insisted was his own initiative, he sent his son-in-law, Lt. John C. Frémont, on a "secret" mission to Oregon in 1843. When Frémont set out from Independence, Mo., in 1843, he was part of a cavalcade of emigrants heading west over the Oregon Trail. Joseph B. Chiles's party had departed for California ahead of him, as had Elijah White's caravan bound for Oregon. Sir William Drummond Stewart headed a large entourage bound for one last hunt on the Green River, while William Gilpin was traveling across the mountains with visions of a transcontinental railroad dancing in his head. Frémont's party was guided by the veteran mountain man Tom "Broken Hand" Fitzpatrick; he was soon joined by two other giants of the fur trade, Kit Carson and

Alexis Godey. In an effort to locate a new trail, Frémont marched out along the Kansas rather than the Platte River, crossed over the Front Range of the Rockies at the head of the Cache de la Poudre River, then trekked over the barren Laramie Plain to the Sweetwater and South Pass. From there he and his men crossed the Wasatch Mountains and gazed upon the Great Salt Lake as it lay before them in "still and solitary grandeur." "The Pathfinder," as he came to be called, described the Salt Lake Valley in such glowing terms that when Brigham Young took his beleaguered Mormons out of Nauvoo, Ill., Frémont's report probably influenced his decision to settle in the deserts of Utah.

Senator Thomas Hart Benton, leading advocate of American expansionism during the first half of the 19th century. He used the explorations of his son-in-law John C. Frémont to buttress his arguments urging settlement of the trans-Mississippi West.

Frémont pushed on, past the British outpost at Fort Hall in Idaho to the Columbia River where he paused at the Dalles. He sent a party on to the mouth of the Columbia and thus technically linked up with the Wilkes expedition, but his mind really was set on turning southward in search of the elusive "Rio Buenaventura." On November 23, 1843, he did just that. He and his men followed the Des Chutes River for a few days, coming out on the northern edge of what Frémont was the first to recognize as the Great Basin. (In fact he gave it that name.) The rest of the journey took them south along the Sierra. In the middle of winter, almost in despair of their lives, he and his men crossed over the Sierra above Lake Tahoe. They finally struggled down from the peaks and followed the American River to Capt. Johann Sutter's new ranch, which Chiles' emigrant party had already reached over an easier route. In crossing the Sierra and descending the American River, Frémont and his men had, of course, walked right over California's main gold region, which in 6 years would be crowded with goldseekers of every description. But the Pathfinder and his men were not exploring for gold; they were primarily interested in California's possibilities for agricultural settlement by Americans. On this account Frémont wrote glowing reports about California as a pastoral paradise.

His return march took him across Tehachapi Pass and over the Old Spanish Trail across the Great Basin desert to within sight of where the modern city of Las Vegas stands today. There he was joined by ex-mountain man Joe Walker, who showed him a short cut across the Colorado River plateau. Then he traveled along the White and Duchesne rivers just below the Uinta Mountains to the Bayou Salade or great South Park of Colorado. This stretch included some of the wildest and

Kit Carson served as a guide on a number of Frémont's expeditions, and the two remained lifelong friends.

least known parts of the western wilderness.

From the parks of Colorado the return journey was over a familiar route via the head of the Arkansas River and Bent's Fort on the Arkansas near the junction of the Purgatory River. On his expedition of 1843-44, Frémont had, in effect, circumnavigated the whole West. Clearly he had not been a pathfinder, but rather a political and scientific explorer. He was searching out the possibilities for an American occupation of the West. With this in mind, and with the substantial aid of Charles Preuss, his Prussian cartographer, he made the first overall map of the West based on accurate astronomical sightings. He also refused to include portions of the West he had not seen, though he made an error in connecting Great Salt Lake with freshwater Utah Lake. He did, however, correctly define and label the immense Great Basin for the first time. This was perhaps his greatest geographical achievement. He also followed up his large comprehensive map with an emigrant map drawn in seven sections by Charles Preuss. This became one of the most important of all maps of the Oregon and California trails because it gave precise distances and detailed information on landmarks, river crossings, grazing lands and Indian tribes. When Frémont submitted his report and maps to Congress they created a sensation and were reprinted and widely distributed. He was the explorer-as-propagandist without equal.

Frémont did not rest on his laurels, however. In the spring of 1845 he headed west again, ostensibly to explore the U.S.-Mexican border country at the headwaters of the Arkansas and Red Rivers. After journeying to the Upper Arkansas, he sent his second-in-command, Lt. James W. Ábert, down the Canadian River with his report. Then, with a tough crew of seasoned mountain men, he headed west across the mountains and the Salt Lake Desert to California. Once in California he bid defiance to Mexican and American authorities alike and put his men to the service of the Bear Flag Revolution.

The war with Mexico introduced a greatly increased number of army explorers into the West. Virtually all of these military explorers were commissioned officers in the Corps of Topographical Engineers, now commanded by Col. John James Ábert who had previously been Frémont's assistant. Every main element of the invading armies under Generals Zachary Taylor, John E. Wool, Stephen Watts Kearny, and Winfield Scott carried a complement of Topographical Engineers who aspired to

Scenes from Frémont's explorations:
Top: *Klamath Lake, California, located by Frémont during his 1845 expedition. From a drawing by Edward M. Kern. It was here that Frémont reportedly received secret instructions from the U.S. Government leading to his involvement in the Bear Flag Revolt.* Center: *Sutter's Fort in 1847, just after the American flag was raised over it for the first time. It was near here a year later that gold was discovered, setting off the great California gold rush of 1849.* Bottom: *Pass in the Sierra Nevada during the winter of 1843-44. From a nearby peak Frémont saw Lake Tahoe for the first time.*

Jefferson Davis of Mississippi was responsible for developing and coordinating the Pacific Railroad Surveys. His advocacy of a Southern route in his final report to Congress led critics to charge that the Surveys were biased from the start.

match Frémont's spectacular success.

The most important work to come out of the war was done by Lt. William H. Emory, who accompanied General Kearny's command to Santa Fe and then west via the Gila River and the Mojave Desert to California. Emory published a detailed report of the march, complete with the first accurate map of the Southwest. His *Notes of a Military Reconnaissance from Fort Leavenworth in Missouri to San Diego in California, Including Parts of the Arkansas, Del Norte, and Gila Rivers* (1848) is a classic of western exploration. In it he made two observations that were to have major importance in western and American history. First he said that much of the Southwest was too arid for individual settlement: no enterprise could survive without cooperation in the distribution of water. Secondly, he declared that "No one who has ever visited this country and who is acquainted with the character and value of slave labor in the United States would ever think of bringing his slaves here with any view to profit . . . ." The latter sentiment, since Emory was a fellow Whig, undoubtedly influenced Daniel Webster's speech on the Compromise of 1850 concerning "the imaginary Negro in an impossible place."

Emory's war experiences made him probably the country's leading expert on the Southwest, and this expertise was soon needed. The treaty ending the Mexican War had drawn a boundary based on geographical ideas that were vague at best, and in some places completely wrong. To correct this, Emory, between 1848 and 1855, was called upon to supervise the demarcation of the United States-Mexican Boundary line from Brownsville on the Rio Grande to San Diego on the Pacific. This was a new kind of exploration—regional exploration on a vast scale. It resulted in the actual laying down of the astronomically determined boundary upon the earth by a system of markers. Most important, it resulted in maps and an extensive regional survey of geology, flora, fauna, archeology and Indian tribes. It also raised the question of the possibility of a southern transcontinental railroad route, which led to the Gadsden Purchase. Thus Emory was a pathfinder for the new age of locomotion and steam.

The most spectacular Army exploration of the period came in 1853, when Secretary of War Jefferson Davis ordered the Topographical Corps into the field to conduct a series of explorations and surveys across the West to determine the most feasible route for a transcontinental railroad. Isaac I. Stephens, seconded by Capt. George

The Pacific Railroad
Reports, *published in 13 volumes, contain some of the best landscape descriptions of the American West during the 1850s. Accompanying the* Reports *was a series of two- and three-color lithographs by a number of individual artists, among them R. H. Kern, John Mix Stanley, F. W. von Egloffstein, H. B. Möllhausen, and Gustave Sohon. Those reproduced here are from the Isaac I. Stevens Survey of 1853-54 and rank among the best of the series. From top to bottom, they show a herd of bison near Lake Jessie in east-central North Dakota, by J. M. Stanley; members of the Survey party crossing the Bitterroot River in western Montana, also by Stanley; and an eastward view of Clark's Fork south of Flathead Lake, by Gustave Sohon.*

75

The Pacific Railroad Surveys
1853–1855

	Stevens 1853–1854		Parke 1853–1855
	Gunnison-Beckwith 1853–1854		Whipple 1853–1854
	Abbott 1853–1855		Pope 1854
			Transcontinental railroad as built

CANADA

Fort Union

MINNESOTA TERRITORY

MICHIGAN

WISCONSIN

St. Paul

NEBRASKA TERRITORY

DAKOTA BADLANDS

Grand River

Missouri River

IOWA

ILLINOIS

Mississippi River

G R E A T

Fort Laramie

North Platte River

MOUNTAINS

South Platte R.

Platte River

Omaha

Council Bluffs

MISSOURI

Illinois River

Republican River

P L A I N S

KANSAS TERRITORY

Smoky Hill River

Kansas R.

Fort Leavenworth

Independence

St. Louis

Osage River

M O U N T A I N S

Arkansas River

Purgatory R.

Cimarron River

ARKANSAS

KY.

TEXAS

Canadian River

UNORGANIZED TERRITORY

Fort Smith

Mississippi River

TENN.

MISS.

Red River

LOUISIANA

Guadalupe Pass

Poster distributed by the Union Pacific Railroad, extolling the virtues of coast-to-coast train travel.

B. McClellan, led a northern survey between the 47th and 49th parallels that sought to connect the Great Lakes with the Pacific Coast. Lt. John W. Gunnison led another party out along the 38th parallel below the Uinta Mountains and far south of the Great Salt Lake. Lt. Amiel Weeks Whipple traversed the 35th parallel west from Santa Fe. And Lts. John G. Parke and John B. Pope worked from each end of a southwestern or 32nd parallel route. Parke and Lt. Henry L. Abbott also explored north and south along the Pacific Coast for a route that would link up the coastal ports with whatever railroads might be built. There were also other parties in the field. Frémont, now resigned from the army, led a party along a line close to his march of 1845, and they almost perished in the deep snows of the southern Rockies. (The great mountain man Bill Williams did perish trying to retrieve their gear.) Also the Texan engineer, Andrew B. Gray, led a State-sponsored survey out across the Pecos River that he hoped would connect up with any line moving west from El Paso del Norte.

Only one great tragedy occurred on the surveys: Lieutenant Gunnison and most of his men were massacred by the Ute Indians on the Sevier River in Utah. Thereupon Lt. Edward G. Beckwith assumed command and traced out a route from Great Salt Lake across to California. He was aided by Capt. Howard Stansbury's careful survey and map of Great Salt Lake in 1849-50.

The result of the Pacific Railroad Surveys in immediate practical terms was nil. Each of the expedition leaders proclaimed his route to the Pacific the "most practicable" one, which left the whole question deadlocked by sectional politics in Congress. Secretary Davis clearly favored the southern route in his final report, but factions split the South as would-be terminal cities all up and down the Mississippi argued for the honor. It was not until the summer of 1866 that James T. Evans, working under the command of Col. Grenville M. Dodge, discovered Lone Tree (now Evans) Pass over the Rocky Mountains and made the Union Pacific portion of a transcontinental railroad possible. A Republican-Unionist Administration under Abraham Lincoln had long since decreed that the route would be a northern one, with its eastern terminus at Omaha across the Mississippi from Council Bluffs. As early as 1860 Californians had determined that Donner Pass was suitable for a railroad over the Sierra, and by July 1, 1862, when the Pacific Railroad Bill was signed into law, Sacramento had been chosen for the western or Central Pacific terminus.

The transcontinental railroad was finally completed on May 10, 1869, when construction crews and dignitaries of the Central Pacific and Union Pacific railroads met and joined track at Promontory, Utah. Over a thousand miles long, and scaling two immense mountain ranges and the vast stretches of the Great Basin, it was the engineering wonder of the age. It was also a significant achievement in the history of exploration—one that has often been overlooked because it was conducted by teams of surveyors and engineers rather than individual military heroes like Frémont.

In addition to the railroad surveys, throughout the 1840s and 1850s army explorers conducted what amounted to a "great reconnaissance" of the American West. Many expeditions crossed the Southwest, for example. In 1849 Lt. James Hervey Simpson led the first expedition since the days of the Spaniards into the Navajo stronghold at Canyon de Chelly. High up on the canyon walls he and his men discovered the lost cliff dwelling of the Anasazi. In 1851 Capt. Lorenzo Sitgreaves trekked across the Southwest just below the Grand Canyon in an early search for a wagon or railroad route. Six years later aboard a prefabricated steamboat Lt. Joseph Christmas Ives chugged up the Colorado River to Black Canyon, then marched overland and down into the Grand Canyon at Diamond Creek. He and his party were the first white men ever to reach the floor of the canyon. Along with his party was the geologist John Strong Newberry who saw the possibilities of such a deep descent into the earth and traced out the first important stratigraphic column in the West. His description of the different layers of earth that he could observe from the canyon floor provided a measuring stick for all future geologists in the West. Ives' report on the expedition was a masterpiece in both literary and scientific terms. Not the least of its contributions, besides Newberry's column, was the first relief map of the West drawn by the Prussian, F.W. von Egloffstein. Hardly had Ives finished his expedition at the Hopi Villages of Oraibi and Moenkopi than Capt. John N. Macomb discovered and described the junction of the Green and the Grand Rivers in western Colorado, thus fitting a key piece into the puzzle of western geography. Macomb and his men also saw abundant remains of the lost Anasazi civilization as they marched along the San Juan River, though they missed the grandest ruin of them all—Mesa Verde.

Capt. James H. Simpson, one of the ablest officers of the Corps of Topographical Engineers. By the time he left the field in 1859, he had marched over more of the West than any other military topographer.

Farther north Lieutenant Simpson crossed the Great Basin once again in search of a railroad route while Capt. William F. Raynolds explored the Dakota Badlands and the Upper Missouri. Along with Raynolds were two paleontologists, Fielding Bradford Meek and Ferdinand V. Hayden, Together they worked out the cretaceous geological horizon of the Dakota country and discovered great caches of extinct animal bones. When they brought their collections back to Philadelphia they provided Dr. Joseph Leidy with the material for the first important book on Western American paleontology, *The Ancient Fauna of Nebraska.* Leidy also found the remains of tiny primitive horses among the collections and published a paper showing how the horse had evolved through time. (This came out just before Charles Darwin published his revolutionary work, *On the Origin of Species.*) And finally, as if to close out exploration in the continental United States just on the eve of the Civil War, Lt. John G. Parke, working with the British Royal Engineers, laid out through the Northwest wilderness the last boundary between the United States and Canada.

All of these expeditions were described in lavishly illustrated reports published by Congress. Taken together the reports represent the most comprehensive body of information about the West up to that time. The centerpiece of all the knowledge realized from Army exploring activity during this era of the "great reconnaissance" was the extraordinary set of 13 volumes generated by the Pacific Railroad Surveys and published between 1854 and 1859. They represented "an encyclopedia of western experience." In addition to the narrative accounts of the individual expeditions, the *Pacific Railroad Reports* also included reports on geology, complete with geologic maps of vast regions; descriptions of plants, animals, birds, and fishes; and an ethnographic report covering most of the Indian tribes of the West. In scientific terms the *Pacific Railroad Reports* dramatically illustrated the advent of specialization and teamwork in the study of a region. Because they were also aimed at determining the possibilities of the whole West for different kinds of settlement they represented a very early and monumental example of ecological study. And finally they represented a cartographical milestone. Each expedition produced a detailed map of the country it traversed. All these were published in the *Reports,* but in addition Lt. Gouverneur Kemble Warren compiled the data from these maps and those of all the other Army expeditions into the first

Simpson's 1859 expedition across Utah's Great Basin resulted in the establishment of more direct emigrant and mail routes between Salt Lake City and California. These watercolors, created by John J. Young from sketches by H. V. A. von Beckh, were part of a series prepared to accompany Simpson's official report. Top: *The expedition crossing the Great Salt Lake Desert, described by Simpson as "a somber, dreary waste, where neither man nor beast can live."* Center: *A habitation of "Go-shoot" (Gosiute) Indians in Pleasant Valley near the present Utah-Nevada border.* Bottom: *The Simpson caravan entering Genoa, a Mormon settlement on the eastern slopes of the Sierra Nevada near Lake Tahoe. Genoa's 150 residents raised the American flag and fired a 13-gun salute to honor the successful completion of the expedition.*

scientifically accurate comprehensive map of the West. After the pioneering work of Lewis and Clark it was perhaps the most important map of the West ever drawn.

In one sense, the era of Army exploration represented a strange phenomenon. As Daniel Boorstin has put it, during this period the West was "settled before it was explored." What this meant, of course, was that each age sought different things from the West, and the development of science and technology refined the questions that explorers sought to answer as each decade passed. During the era of Army exploration questions shifted dramatically from those of the fur trader and farmer to those of the gold seeker, townbuilder, and railroad entrepreneur, as California suddenly filled with 300,000 people and Colorado threatened to do the same.

Members of the Hayden Survey take sightings from atop Colorado's Sultan Mountain with a theodolite, an instrument which measures horizontal and vertical angles.

The Great Post-Civil War Surveys

The relatively sudden peopling of California as a result of the gold Rush stimulated a whole new era of exploration in the West. This era was dominated by great government-sponsored surveys that covered hundreds of square miles of territory and produced explorers of great daring and intelligence who served in public employ. As early as 1860 California hired Josiah Dwight Whitney, a Yale Phi Beta Kappa trained in Europe, to lead a survey team that was to explore the whole State in search of mineral resources. Whitney, however, saw his task as larger than "a mere prospecting expedition." He landed in San Francisco intent upon making a thorough scientific study of California, including its complex geology as well as its flora and fauna. As such, his work would provide a model for all future surveys in the great West. For the next decade (all through the Civil War) he and a crack team of naturalist-explorers carefully mapped California's varied and complex terrain from Death Valley in the south to Lassen's Peak in the north. His team included William H. Brewer, James Terry Gardner, and Clarence King, all also of Yale. None of them were tenderfeet for long, however. With incredible diligence and daring they clambered up and down the highest peaks of the Sierras, scaled the walls of Yosemite, braved 118-degree heat to map the deserts of the south and even descended into the frightening mines of the Comstock Lode. Whitney himself was set upon by highwaymen; Brewer and his parties on many occasions arrived back at base camp ragged and starving. King, however, was

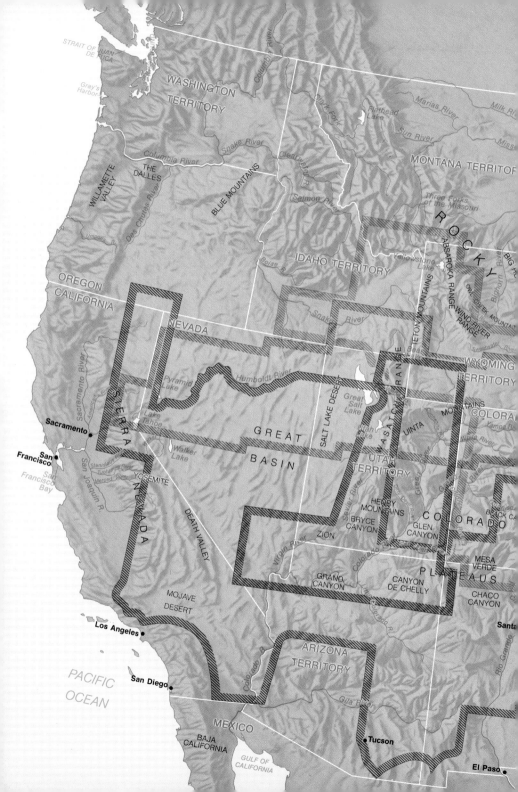

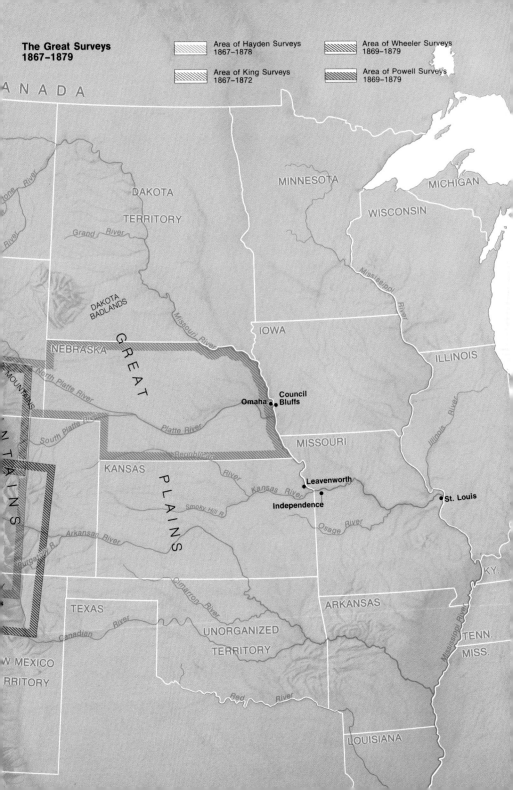

**The Great Surveys
1867–1879**

Area of Hayden Surveys
1867–1878

Area of King Surveys
1867–1872

Area of Wheeler Surveys
1869–1879

Area of Powell Surveys
1869–1879

CANADA

DAKOTA

TERRITORY

Grand River

MINNESOTA

MICHIGAN

WISCONSIN

Missouri River

Yellowstone River

River

DAKOTA
BADLANDS

NEBRASKA

GREAT

North Platte River

MOUNTAINS

South Platte River

Platte River

IOWA

ILLINOIS

Mississippi

River

Omaha • Council
Bluffs

Illinois River

N T A I N S

Republican

KANSAS

PLAINS

River

Kansas River

MISSOURI

Leavenworth

Smoky Hill R.

Independence

Arkansas River

Osage River

St. Louis

urgeon R.

Arkansas River

KY.

Cimarron

River

TEXAS

UNORGANIZED

ARKANSAS

Canadian River

TERRITORY

TENN.

MISS.

W MEXICO

RRITORY

Red River

LOUISIANA

the most flamboyant of all. He was a new style of mountain man. Imbued with the Alpine or mountain climber's temperment just then emerging in Europe, King, whenever he could, made for "the top of California"—the highest peaks he could find. He scaled Lassen's lonely blue cone, and in 1864 after a series of harrowing adventures among the ice fields and awful gorges of the upper Kern River country, he climbed and named Mount Tyndall, which he thought to be the highest mountain in California—until he looked away in the distance over the jagged peaks and saw Mt. Whitney. It was years before he could climb that peak but he did not rest until he had done so. All of these adventures he vividly described in his western classic, *Mountaineering in the Sierra Nevada* (1872).

By 1870 Whitney and his men had completed a modern scientific survey of California. They had mapped the whole State for the first time, and had untangled its complex geology. They had surveyed all of the known mineral deposits and examined the possibilities for agriculture. Whitney's two scientific works, *Geology of California* and *The Auriferous Gravels of California* were classics, while his *Yosemite Book* matched Clarence King's *Mountaineering in the Sierra Nevada* as an introduction to the wonders and beauties of the state. In the course of their labors, too, Whitney and his men used their influence in Washington to persuade President Abraham Lincoln to grant the Yosemite Valley to California for a public park. Lincoln did so in 1864, thereby setting the precedent for the national wilderness park idea, which became a unique American contribution to civilization.

But all did not go well with Whitney's survey. The California legislature did not find him diligent enough in locating mineral deposits—and they failed to recognize that terms like "auriferous gravels" meant gold-bearing strata. They chided him and his men for being eastern "dudes" and "dandies" and Whitney especially for falling prey to the "Calaveras Skull Hoax." In the latter case, two drunken miners had planted an Indian skull deep in the base of a mine shaft, and Whitney was led to believe that it was the remains of an extinct, pre-historic man. All California laughed. But no one laughed when Yale chemist Benjamin Silliman pointed out that Whitney and his men had overlooked immense deposits of oil in and around Santa Barbara. This was inexcusable. No matter that the oil discovered was not commercially usable, that three companies floated by Silliman were declared fraudulent, that Silliman as a result was dismissed from the Yale faculty and drummed out of the world of serious science forever. What mattered was that the "dudes" had missed a "main chance" for wealth-seeking Californians. By 1870 Whitney's survey was dead. "Oil has done us in," he wrote mournfully to his brother back in New Haven, Conn. Yet the California Survey produced a prototype for the great surveys that provided the institutional form for the exploration of the West after the Civil War.

However scientifically organized exploration became in this period, it did not preclude feats of individual adventuring. In May 1869 one-armed Maj. John Wesley Powell and nine volunteers set off down the Green River in an effort to explore the last completely unknown major river in the United States—the mighty Colorado of the West. For 92 days Powell and his men braved the river in four small boats, never knowing what to expect.

John Wesley Powell, geologist, teacher, and explorer, led the first expedition down the Colorado River through the Grand Canyon in 1869.

They cut right through the Uintas on foaming cataracts, passed through the flaming gorges of Lodore Canyon, cruised placidly for a time past the Yampa River country, paused awestruck before the intricately carved formations at the junction of the Grand (now the main branch of the Colorado) with the Green, shot through Glen Canyon and the awful treacherous rapids of Marble Canyon, and entered into the majesty of the Grand Canyon itself with its cliffs towering well over a mile above them and the waters foaming and crashing over boulders and cataracts. By the time Powell finally emerged at Callville, a Mormon settlement below the canyon, he had been given up for dead by virtually every newspaper editor in the country. Indeed, he had lost two boats, one man had deserted early at the Ute Indian Agency, and three others attempting to climb out of the Grand Canyon were killed by Indians. But the expedition survived; the Colorado and the Grand Canyon no longer were mysteries; and along the way they had discovered the last unknown river (the Dirty Devil) and the last unknown mountain range (the Henry) in the American West.

Powell's trip was more than a stunt, however. He was a serious scientific explorer, so serious that in the summer of 1871 he made the hazardous trip again, mapping and surveying the route carefully and giving a name to the whole canyon country—the Colorado Plateau Region. Powell's team became a survey group, "The United States Geological and Geographical Survey of the Rocky Mountains," operating first under the Smithsonian Institution, then under the Department of the Interior. As Powell saw it, the first task was the mapping of the whole Colorado River region. This he placed in charge of his brother-in-law Almon H. Thompson and a young apprentice, Frederick Dellenbaugh. He also employed a photographer, E. O. Beaman from Salt Lake City, to capture the stupendous sights on wet plate, glass negatives. Beaman soon left the wilderness, however, and his place was taken by Jack Hillers, who became one of the great photographers of the early West.

Powell had two main concerns. He was intensely interested in the mechanics of just how the Colorado Plateau and the Colorado River had come about. In this instance he was asking an almost revolutionary question for geologists of his time: how exactly did nature work? His second concern related to the possibilities for settlement in what obviously was an arid region. To answer his theoretical question, Powell assembled still another team, some of whose members should not be forgotten—Clarence Dutton, Grove Karl Gilbert and William H. Holmes—who explored the high plateaus of Utah, including Zion and Bryce Canyons, the Henry and Uinta Mountains, and the Colorado Plateau. In so doing they put together a complete picture of the way in which the Colorado Plateau was uplifted through eons while the Colorado River steadily cut down through layer upon layer of rock strata, carving out the beautiful and intricate canyons and "denuding" the great Colorado Plateau over a thousand square miles. Powell's reports and those of his scientific compatriots, especially Dutton and Gilbert, together formed a model of the process of uplift and erosion on a gigantic scale that had applicability anywhere in the world. They had added the science of mechanics to geology which had heretofore been an historical study of the age of the earth.

Because of these studies Powell had a clearer answer to his second question. In 1878 he published *A Report Upon Lands of the Arid Regions of the United States,* one of the most important books ever produced by an American. In it he called for restraint on the headlong settlement of the West and the wasting of scarce resources. The arid regions would not support the traditional family farm, he said, because water placed limits on all settlement and forced cooperation. Moreover, all the western lands needed to be classified according to potentially efficient use—farming lands, grazing lands, timber lands, mineral lands—and careful planning exercised through voluntary cooperation at every stage of settlement. If sodbusters, cattlemen, and greedy mining magnates had listened to Powell there would have been far less feuding in the Gilded Age West, a new and better Homestead Act, and far more resources left for future generations. John Wesley Powell was an explorer-turned-scientific prophet and reformer. The adventure of his canyon voyage turned out to have a further major impact on the country when he helped establish the U.S. Geological Survey in 1879.

Meanwhile, in the late 1860s and 1870s, several other survey teams of explorers were combing the West. The irrepressible Clarence King had secured War Department support for a bold project—the U.S. Survey of the Fortieth Parallel. Beginning in 1867, when he left the California Survey, King and a team explored and mapped a great 100-mile swath across the West from the Sierra to the Front Range of the Rockies along the route of the proposed transcontinental railroad. Every year from 1867 to 1872 King had men in the field mapping the country, studying its geology, looking for gold and silver deposits, collecting plants and animals—essentially engaging in every kind of endeavor that would indicate to the government the utility of the land across which the railroad would pass and on which presumably settlements would spring up. Always the adventurer, King chased down robbers and deserters, crawled into caves after grizzly bears, and scaled all the high mountains. He even managed to get himself struck by lightning, turning one half of his body brown for nearly a week. There is not room to recount the individual adventures of King and his men of the Fortieth Parallel Survey. Suffice it to say that out in the arid wastes of the Great Basin or atop the highest peaks of the central Rockies they braved many of the same dangers of the earlier mountain men of Jedediah Smith's generation. King's work, like Powell's, had both theoretical and practical significance. His *Systematic Geology* masterfully reconstructed the entire geologic history of the West while his co-workers' monograph, *The Mining Industry,* became the definitive work on that vital subject. (Unlike Whitney, King would not see his survey fail for want of attention to mining, which was of the greatest interest to western speculators.) And in 1873, as if to dramatize his own interest in this all-important subject and the utility of science, King exposed one of the West's greatest frauds—the Great Diamond Hoax. Two confidence men had salted a mesa with

Clarence King, surveyor of the Fortieth Parallel, 1867-72, introduced into mapping the system of denoting topography by using contour lines. He also helped organize the U. S. Geological Survey, becoming its first director in 1879.

Nathaniel P. Langford (top) and Henry D. Washburn led the first full-scale exploring expedition into the Yellowstone region in 1870. Langford later claimed credit for being the first to urge creation of Yellowstone as a national park. He was the park's first superintendent. Right: "The Grand Canyon of the Yellowstone," from the painting by Thomas Moran, 1872.

diamonds and persuaded San Francisco and eastern investors that the land could be theirs for $600,000. Pocketing the money, the confidence men disappeared. King, acutely aware of the California oil fraud, was suspicious. Through careful detective work involving his knowledge of the geology and geography of the Rocky Mountain region, King and his men (almost rivalling Sherlock Holmes and Dr. Watson) found the diamond mesa, which the speculators had kept secret, determined it to be salted, and exposed the hoax, thereby saving investors across the nation millions. Nothing did more to credit the scientific explorer in the Gilded Age than King's feat of detective work.

Throughout the 1870s the army continued to explore and re-explore the West. Individual expeditions were sent out under the authority of various commands, and some turned out to be important. In 1870 under the urging of Nathaniel P. Langford, the army supplied a military escort for an expedition into the still little-known Yellowstone region. The civilian party was led by Henry D. Washburn and Langford himself, while the escort was led by Lt. Gustavus Doane. They entered the Yellowstone Park area in late August 1870 and immediately were dazzled by its marvels. As they passed by the painted pools, stupendous canyons, and spurting geysers, the men of the Washburn-Doane expedition named them all and together determined to see to it that the whole region became a national park. Langford (soon to be called "National Park" Langford) worked ceaselessly at the project. Lieutenant Doane's map defined the area, and the military expedition of Capt. John Whitney Barlow the following year helped push the proposal forward.

The army mounted its most extensive exploring operation far to the west and south. This was Lt. George Montague Wheeler's "United States Geographical Surveys West of the One Hundredth Meridian." Wheeler, who had graduated from West Point in 1866, too late to make his mark in the Civil War, yearned to emulate the pre-war feats of the Army Topographical engineer explorers. Attached to Gen. Edward O. C. Ord's command in California, Wheeler spent the years 1867 to 1870 exploring and mapping the deserts of the Great Basin south of Clarence King's Fortieth Parallel Survey. By 1871 the army had become interested in the Colorado River as a means of supplying its garrisons in the central Rockies. Wheeler, as chief of the army surveys west of the 100th meridian, headed south from Halleck Station

on the Central Pacific Railroad in May 1871. He divided his survey up into teams which zigzagged south, east, and west across Nevada, mapping enormous amounts of territory. Three of Wheeler's parties, including one he led himself, struggled across the furnace-hot wastes of Death Valley, making the definitive map of that future national monument. But Wheeler's most spectacular feat was his expedition by boat *up* the Colorado River and into Grand Canyon as far as Diamond Creek, the point reached by Lt. Joseph Ives in 1857.

After his Grand Canyon expedition in 1871 Wheeler realized that, as he put it, "the day of the pathfinder has sensibly ended," and he organized his men into survey teams who mapped the West beyond the 100th meridian in a series of quadrants similar to those later used by the U.S. Geological Survey. Despite bureaucratic clashes with civilian scientific parties under Powell and especially Ferdinand V. Hayden, by 1879 when his survey was terminated Wheeler had mapped almost one-third of the country west of the 100th meridian. He had devised the contour map and produced in all some 71 maps of the West. He had studied the Comstock Lode and the Grand Canyon in detail and his photographer, Timothy O'Sullivan, had taken spectacular photographs of the Grand Canyon Expedition. In the end, however, Wheeler's work proved to be the "last stand" of the army explorer in the West. His survey gave way to the civilian-controlled U.S. Geological Survey in 1879.

The last of the Great Surveys, the one led by Ferdinand V. Hayden, was also in a sense the first of the surveys. Before the Civil War, Hayden and his partner, Fielding B. Meek, a paleontologist, had explored the Dakota Badlands with various army expeditions. At the close of the war, Hayden began a State survey of Nebraska. His work so pleased Congress that in 1869 he was given a large appropriation and made head of the "United States Geological Survey of the Territories." Hayden was a good theoretical geologist but his eye was on the practical. The purpose of his expeditions to the Rocky Mountains was to find coal and other minerals; consequently he was always well supported by Congress as well as local western interests. In addition to his interest in western minerals, Hayden also was one of the first to see the West as the land of the nature-loving tourist. His expedition into the Yellowstone geyser region in 1871 resulted in spectacular photographs by William H. Jackson, breathtaking panoramic drawings by the young topographer William H. Holmes, and grand Ruskinian renditions of Yellowstone's marvelous features by Thomas Moran, the country's foremost landscape painter.

Hayden, like Doane and Barlow earlier, was overwhelmed by the "grandeur and beauty" of the Yellowstone region. Drawing upon the precedent set by the Yosemite Act of 1864, Hayden promoted a Yellowstone Park bill in Washington in late 1871 and early 1872. On March 1, 1872, following a surprisingly easy passage by Congress, the bill was signed into law by President Ulysses S. Grant and the first national park was born.

The Yellowstone expedition made Hayden famous, but perhaps his most important work was the detailed exploration and mapping of mountainous Colorado. Here his teams worked through some of the ruggedest country in the West to complete the masterful *Atlas of Colorado.* They also discovered one of the great symbolic wonders of the West — the Mount of the Holy Cross, a high peak in western Colorado across the face of which snow had formed a mammoth cross. When the explorers first stumbled across a shoulder of Notch Mountain and the Mount of the Holy Cross burst into view with a shining radiance, a rainbow also formed a kind of halo about the mountain and its cross. To them and to countless thousands who saw Moran's painting and Jackson's photographs, the mountain was the epitome of God smiling down upon the sublime, unspoiled beauty of the American West.

Hayden's men, notably the photographer Jackson and the artist Holmes, made one other important discovery. In 1874 while surveying the San Juan River country in southern Colorado, they turned up Mancos Canyon and there, high up on the canyon walls, they saw ancient cliff dwellings of the long vanished Indian civilization called by contemporary Indians the Anasazi or "the Ancient Ones." For the next 2 years Jackson and Holmes led expeditions into Mancos Canyon and other ancient pueblo sites in Chaco Canyon, Canyon de Chelly, and the three sacred mesas of the Hopi. In their careful work they revealed a lost horizon of ancient civilization to Gilded Age America. Models of the Anasazi ruins were one of the features of the Philadelphia Centennial Exhibition of 1876.

But despite the spectacular work of Hayden and his men, his survey too came to an end in 1879. All of the Great Surveys — those of Powell, King, Hayden, and Wheeler — were consolidated into one great bureau, the U.S. Geological Survey. For a time, King became its

chief, then Powell assumed the directorship and brought it to national prominence. Under Powell the exploration of the West was organized as never before and related most directly to the great national problem of how best to utilize the resources of the West for the American people. Science and management techniques had seemingly replaced the great day of the individual explorer. The year 1879 appeared to mark the end of the individual explorer's frontier just as surely as the census report of 1890 perhaps prematurely announced the end of the settler's frontier.

Spectacular discovery, if not the urge for exploration, did not really die with the Great Surveys in 1879 however. On a wintery December day in 1888, for instance, a cowboy named Richard Wetherill and his sidekick Charlie Mason, looking for wandering cattle, climbed out upon a windswept point in Mesa Verde and, looking down into a deep valley, they saw, like a "mirage" in the falling snow—the Cliff Palace, its walls, towers and turrets undisturbed perhaps for centuries. It stunned their imaginations, and Wetherill dedicated his life to untangling the secrets of Mesa Verde. Year after year he discovered more ruins tucked away in the high places. Then he fanned out over the whole San Juan country, discovering countless other ruins like Kiet Siel and Grand Gulch. Eventually he built a house adjoining the massive Pueblo Bonito ruin at Chaco Canyon, living there until his death in 1910.

But the death of Richard Wetherill is not the end of the story. A whole generation of archeologists followed in his footsteps. Thus one age of exploration has succeeded another and, despite the superhighway, the proliferation of ski lodges, and endless sprouting of strip culture towns and burgeoning cities that all look like Los Angeles, the West remains a place to be explored, whether on the cosmic scale of satellite and heat-sensitive camera, or on the still practical human scale of the individual for whom each canyon, each river, each remaining patch of wilderness will still yield the wonder of discovery.

William H. Goetzmann

Cliff Palace, Mesa Verde, discovered by cowboys Richard Wetherill and Charlie Mason in 1888. Although other Mesa Verde cliff dwellings had been discovered as early as 1874-75, the Cliff Palace group was by far the largest and most impressive.

Part 3

The documentary record of 19th century exploring activity in the trans-Mississippi West is remarkably complete. The written record, the largest of all, consists of published and unpublished diaries, journals, official reports, correspondence, and field notes filling hundreds of volumes on library shelves and thousands of dusty storage boxes in archival collections across the country. Just as impressive, though not nearly so large, is the pictorial record created by artists, cartographers, and photographers which complements and sometimes expands on the written sources.

Some of the most vivid, colorful, and, in some cases, only record of the early trans-Mississippi West comes from the sketch pads and canvasses of the artists who, either as part of organized exploring expeditions or on their own as travelers, drew and painted what they saw or experienced. Expeditionary cartographers, faced with the challenge of describing new scientific and geological discoveries that could not otherwise be easily explained, did so in the form of maps, charts, graphs, artificially contrived panoramas, and various kinds of landform drawings which, according to one historian, "resemble modern paintings." And when photography became a more portable medium in the 1860s, western survey leaders were quick to embrace it, not only as a way of guaranteeing greater accuracy in documenting their work but as a means of bringing their activities and the wonders of the West to the attention of the public and the Congress, upon whom they depended for support and appropriations.

All in all, the pictorial record of trans-Mississippi exploration between 1803 and 1879 is a rich and varied source of firsthand observation by highly qualified observers. Part of that record, a sampling only, appears on the following pages.

An unknown photographer perches precariously atop Glacier Point to compose a panorama of Yosemite Valley. Landscape photographer William Henry Jackson once said that successful photography requires "labor, patience, and moral stamina." He should have included "courage" in his list. Preceding pages: *Artist Albert Bierstadt is photographed by Eadweard Muybridge while sketching Indians in Yosemite in 1872. For a reproduction of the painting that resulted from this sketching session, see page 103.*

The Artists

They came with the same sense of adventure and uncertainty that motivated the scientists and engineers, and they faced the same heat, cold, wind, rain, and dust. Some were self-taught, some were trained in the best European tradition, and, while what they recorded was influenced by individual psychological, social, and esthetic values, all strove to document as accurately as possible the new land and people they encountered.

Their numbers were legion, and only a few can be men-tioned here. Two Philadelphians, Samuel Seymour and Titian Ramsay Peale (son of Charles), were the first of many artists to accompany an official U.S. Government exploring expedition. Joining Stephen Long on his trek to the Rockies in 1820, they provided the first views of the Indians, animals, and geography of that region. Another Pennsylvanian, George Catlin, made several journeys up the Missouri River in the 1830s intent on studying and painting the Plains Indians before white influence changed them forever. Swiss artist Karl Bodmer, who traveled up the Missouri in 1833-34 with his patron Prince Maximilian, painted some of the same Indians as Catlin, but with more precision. He also created a number of Upper Missouri landscapes that are still unrivaled in many respects.

In 1837 Baltimore artist Alfred Jacob Miller, the first artist to travel the Oregon Trail, chronicled the dying world of the mountain man. Six years later, John James Audubon spent 8 months painting animals along the

Five artists who left an invaluable record of the 19th century West. Left: *George Catlin, from the 1849 portrait by English artist William H. Fisk.* Above: *Alfred Jacob Miller, self-portrait.* Right, top: *Albert Bierstadt, 1859.* Right, bottom: *Karl Bodmer, from a photograph late in life.* Far right: *Thomas Moran in his Newark, N. J., studio in the mid-1870s.*

Missouri River for his "Quadrapeds of North America" series. Canadian artist Paul Kane, deeply affected by Catlin's Indian gallery, journeyed beyond the Rocky Mountains in 1845-48 and filled his sketchbooks with notes and drawings of Indians, fur posts, and Northwest landscapes. And far down in the Southwest, topographical artist Seth Eastman sketched the Texas countryside and its architecture while Richard Kern, one of three brothers to serve as artists on various expeditions, made a significant contribution to scientific knowledge with his drawings of the Navajo stronghold in Canyon de Chelly.

Throughout the 1840s and 1850s artists such as the Kern brothers, John Mix Stanley, Gustave Sohon, John J. Young, F. W. Egloffstein, H. B. Möllhausen, Charles Coppel, and Albert Bierstadt, among others, accompanied and helped to document the various exploring expeditions and railroad surveys conducted by the U.S. Army's Corps of Topographical Engineers. When the great geological surveys of King, Hayden, Wheeler, and Powell took the field in the late 1860s and 1870s, several distinguished landscape painters, including John Henry Hill, Sanford Robinson Gifford, and Thomas Moran, occasionally went along as guest artists. Though they had no official duties, because by then the pictorial record of the surveys was maintained by photographers, these artists were looked upon as effective publicizers of what the *Rocky Mountain News* called "the most remarkable scenery."

The Artists

1 *Mandan Village, 1832, by George Catlin. Catlin's paintings and drawings of Mandan life and culture, including religious and ceremonial rituals never before witnessed by an outsider, provide the main documentation for this primitive Indian tribe that was almost exterminated by small pox in 1837.* 2 *Buffalo and elk along the Upper Missouri River, 1833, by Karl Bodmer, whose paintings and sketches have long been acclaimed for their accurate depiction of people and places of the early trans-Mississippi West.* 3 *Fort William, the first Fort Laramie, 1837, by Alfred Jacob Miller. For an interior view of the fort, see page 62.* 4 *"Indians in Council, California, 1872." Detail from the painting by Albert Bierstadt. Unlike his western landscapes, which have been criticized for being too grandiose and contrived, Bierstadt's Indian studies demonstrate a preciseness and attention to detail that give them a documentary quality. For Eadweard Muybridge's photograph of Bierstadt making sketches for this painting, see pages 96-97.*

1

2

3

4

The Artists

"The Chasm of the Colorado," by Thomas Moran, 1874. Moran called it "the most awfully grand and impressive scene that I have ever yet seen. Above and around us rose a wall of 2000 feet and below us a vast chasm 2500 feet in perpendicular depth and ½ a mile wide. At the bottom the river very muddy and seemingly only a hundred feet wide seemed slowly moving along but in reality is a rushing torrent filled with rapids. A suppressed sort of roar comes up constantly from the chasm but with that exception everything impresses you with an awful stillness." Moran based the painting on sketches he made during his 1873 journey down the Colorado with John Wesley Powell's survey team.

The Mapmakers

The work of the 19th-century explorers of the trans-Mississippi West, as John Noble Wilford points out, "encompassed the broad range of exploratory mapping—from discovery and pathfinding to the charting of rivers and railroad routes, the filling in of spaces on the map that had been blank, and searching for resources. Their maps projected a hitherto unknown world on the minds of the known world. Their best maps replaced geographical lore with geographical reality." The earliest maps of the trans-Mississippi area were those generated by the expeditions of Lewis and Clark and Zebulon Pike along the northern and southern fringes of the Louisiana Purchase and of Stephen Long to the Rocky Mountains. Though crude by later cartographic standards, these maps nevertheless provided the first reliable geographical information on previously unknown lands and formed a basis on which to build what Bernard DeVoto called the "westering" spirit of the Nation.

More accurate and scientific mapping techniques were introduced after the Corps of Topographical Engineers took over the bulk of western exploration in 1838. Over the next 20 years expeditions under such topographical officers as John C. Frémont, William H. Emory, Amiel Weeks Whipple, James H. Simpson, Howard Stansbury, and John W. Gunnison helped to establish national boundaries, wagon trails, and railroad routes. In the process they collected a wealth of scientific and topographic data which made possible the creation of the first comprehensive map of the trans-

Mississippi area.

The result was Lt. Gouverneur K. Warren's general map of the West, based not only on the field reconnaissances of the topographical corps but on explorations by Lewis and Clark and others, including information obtained from trappers and traders. Completed in 1857, Warren's map was so thorough that Carl Wheat, noted historian of trans-Mississippi cartography, concludes that "subsequent efforts in the way of maps may properly be deemed merely filling in the detail." Much of the filling-in was done between 1867 and 1879 by the King, Hayden, Wheeler, and Powell surveys, which laid the scientific foundations of American geological, topographic, and land classification mapping. The surveys also introduced a new type of mapping technique reflected in the work of such artist-topographers as William H. Holmes (left), whose panoramas convey a vivid impression of western landscapes, like that of the Kaibab division of the Grand Canyon shown below.

The Mapmakers

Shown here are four of the most significant maps to result from 19th century exploring activities. **1** William Clark's master map of the West, which has been called "one of the most important maps ever made in America." Clark began it in 1810 and constantly updated it with information supplied by trappers, traders, and travelers on the Upper Missouri. **2** The Frémont-Gibbs-Smith map, which is the only known map showing the extent of the knowledge of western geography that Jedediah Smith accumulated as a result of his various travels. **3** Lt. Gouverneur K. Warren's 1857 Map of the Territory of the United States from the Mississippi to the Pacific Ocean. The first sophisticated map of the trans-Mississippi West, it accompanied Secretary of War Jefferson Davis' final report to Congress on the results of the Pacific Railroad surveys. **4** Lt. George M. Wheeler's 1876 map of the progress of his U. S. Geological Survey West of the 100th Meridian, which shows for the first time a division of the West into quadrants similar to those later used by the U. S. Geological Survey.

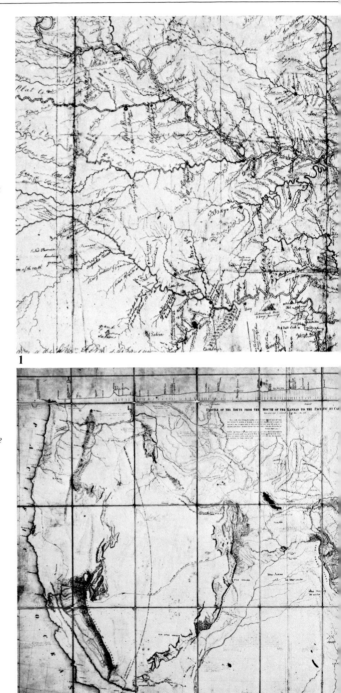

1

2

3

4

The Photographers

Photographic documentation of western exploring expeditions began on a broad scale with the great post-Civil War surveys of Clarence King, Ferdinand V. Hayden, George M. Wheeler, and John Wesley Powell. Leaders of earlier expeditions, notably John Frémont, Isaac I. Stevens, Lt. Joseph C. Ives, and Lt. James H. Simpson, made attempts to create a photographic record of their work, but the process was so slow and in other ways inadequate that little was accomplished. Simpson was so disappointed in the results of his efforts that he flatly concluded that "the camera is not adapted to explorations in the field, and a good artist, who can sketch readily and accurately, is much to be preferred." It took the development of the collodion wet-plate process and the portable, if cumbersome, view-type camera on the eve of the Civil War to finally make expeditionary photography feasible.

King, Hayden, Wheeler, and Powell were all strong advocates of photography, not only as a means of documenting their work but also as a form of publicity to help convince a sometimes reluctant Congress to continue appropriations. For this reason, they insisted on and obtained the services of some of the best landscape photographers in the country. The record they produced, ranging from mountains, deserts, canyons, rivers, lakes, and waterfalls to the great geysers of Yellowstone, not only served to supplement the final reports of the surveys but told the story to thousands of people who might never read it.

Three of the photographers who accompanied the Great Surveys. Above: William Henry Jackson kneels at the edge of a cliff in the Teton Mountains during the 1872 Hayden Survey. Right, top: Timothy O'Sullivan, photographer for the King and Wheeler surveys, poses in Panama during his service with the U. S. Navy expedition to the Isthmus of Darien in 1870. Right: John K. Hillers, Powell's photographer, in the field in Utah, 1872.

One of the most popular type of photographs during this period, and one that Survey photographers produced in great numbers, was the stereograph, which, when viewed through the hand-held stereoscope, created a three-dimensional image. For many it was the next best thing to being there. The stereograph at left was made by Timothy O'Sullivan at the start of the 1871 Wheeler expedition up the Colorado River.

1 Focusing cloth
2 Sensitizing box
3 Processing tank
4 Chemical bottles

The wet-plate camera and equipment shown at left are typical of those used by Survey photographers. They would also have used a portable dark-room tent (either walk-in or tripod-mounted) or an enclosed horse-drawn wagon equipped for sensitizing and processing their photographic plates.

111

Photographs from the Building of the Transcontinental Railroad

The construction of the transcontinental railroad from Omaha, Nebraska, to Sacramento, California, during the last half of the 1860s was the greatest engineering feat that Americans had undertaken. The joining of the Central Pacific and the Union Pacific Railroads at the little town of Promontory, Utah Territory, on May 10, 1869, ushered in a new era in the history of the West. As the rails inched westward, a number of photographers worked along the route, creating an impressive record of the work, a sampling of which appears on these pages. The leaders of the Great Surveys used photographers in much the same fashion. **1** Donner Pass and Lake from above Summit Tunnel in the Sierra Nevada, circa 1868. The snowsheds at right cover exposed sections of Central Pacific track. **2** CP rail bending crew in Ten Mile Canyon, along the Humboldt River, 1868. **3** A Union Pacific train crosses the temporary trestle near Citadel Rock at Green River, Wyoming, late in 1868. **4** UP's construction boss, Gen. John S. Casement, stands beside his supply train near end of track in Wyoming, 1868. The wagon at right is photographer A. J. Russell's traveling darkroom. **5** Chief engineers Samuel S. Montague, left, of the Central Pacific and Grenville M. Dodge of the Union Pacific shake hands following the joining of the rails on May 10, 1869. The most famous of all western railroad photographs, by A. J. Russell.

1

2

3

4

5

Photographs from the King Survey

The first of the Great Surveys of the West was the United States Geological Exploration of the Fortieth Parallel under the direction of Yale-trained geologist Clarence King. Begun in western Nevada on July 3, 1867, and continuing annually for the next 5 years, the King Survey examined and mapped the topography and geology of a 100-mile-wide strip of land along the proposed route of the transcontinental railroad from the eastern slopes of the Sierra Nevada to the Front Range of the Rockies. These photographs in Utah and Idaho were taken by Timothy O'Sullivan, who worked for King from 1867 to 1869. **1** Summits of the Uinta Mountains, Utah, 1869. **2** Wasatch Mountains, Lone Peak Summit, Utah, 1869. King named the peaks and lakes of the Uinta and Wasatch ranges after his sister and her friends. **3** Horseshoe Canyon, Green River, south of Flaming Gorge, Utah, 1868. **4** Salt Lake City, Utah, 1869. **5** Clarence King in a characteristic pose, 1867. **6** Shoshone Falls, from the south bank of the Snake River, southern Idaho, 1868. O'Sullivan called this "one of the most sublime of the Rocky Mountain scenes."

1

2

3

4

5

6

115

Photographs from the Hayden Survey

The United States Geological Survey of the Territories headed by Ferdinand V. Hayden was the biggest and best-known of the Great Surveys. From 1867 to 1878 Hayden and his men explored and catalogued the natural resources of Nebraska, Colorado, Wyoming, and Montana. Among their accomplishments were the creation of the Geological and Geographical Atlas of Colorado (containing panoramic views by artist-topographer William H. Holmes), the discoveries of Colorado's Mount of the Holy Cross and Mesa Verde's ancient cliff dwellings, and the first official and extensive exploration of the Grand Teton region. Hayden, one of the few explorers to view the West as a tourist's paradise, was also one of the first to publicize the grandeur of the Yellowstone area. William Henry Jackson's photographs, some of which are shown here and on the following two pages, supported many of Hayden's ideas. 1 The Mount of the Holy Cross, August 24, 1873. 2 One of the first Mesa Verde cliff dwellings discovered by the Hayden Survey in 1874. John Moss, who led the Hayden party to the ruins, stands at left while journalist Ernest Ingersoll makes notes. 3 The Hayden Survey enroute to the valley of the Yellowstone in 1871. Hayden is mounted second from the right.

1

3

2

117

Hayden and Yellowstone National Park

One of the results of the Hayden Survey was the establishment in 1872 of the Yellowstone region as the first national park. In his later years Hayden tended to claim full credit for the park's creation. Though this claim has long-since been disproven, it is true that without Hayden's vigorous lobbying on behalf of the park's establishment, and William Henry Jackson's Yellowstone photographs (a selection of which appears here), Congress might never have passed the necessary legislation. **1** Mammoth Hot Springs. The figure in the picture is artist Thomas Moran. **2** Old Faithful in eruption while members of the Hayden Survey look on. **3** Yellowstone Lake. **4** Lower Falls of the Yellowstone.

1

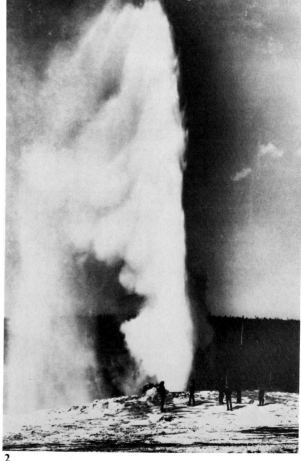

2

3

4

Photographs from the Wheeler Survey

1

Lt. George M. Wheeler's United States Geographical Survey West of the 100th Meridian was created to maintain the Army's presence in survey activities otherwise dominated by civilians, particularly Clarence King and Ferdinand Hayden. Associated with Wheeler as official photographer (and, at times, co-leader) during 1871 and again in 1873 and 1874 was Timothy O'Sullivan, who had earlier worked for King's 40th Parallel Survey. Many of the lithographs that accompanied the Survey's final reports were derived from O'Sullivan's photographs and Wheeler often commended his work. William Henry Jackson called O'Sullivan "one of the best of the government photographers." **1** *Death Valley, 1871, where heat and lack of water brought the Survey to near-disaster while exploring this vast desert land.* **2** *The Colorado River from the rim of the Grand Canyon near Devil's Anvil, 1871. Wheeler was delighted with O'Sullivan's views of the Grand Canyon, calling the whole series "fine" and "interesting and instructive."* **3** *Camp of the Wheeler Survey near Belmont, Nevada, 1871.* **4** *Mohave Indians of the lower Colorado River area. O'Sullivan thought the tribe "the finest specimens in all the West."* **5** *Ruins of White House, Canyon de Chelly, 1873.*

2

3

4

5

Photographs from the Powell Survey

One of the great feats of western exploration was John Wesley Powell's expedition down the Colorado River in 1869. As a result of this adventure, Powell was placed in charge of what would become the United States Geological and Geographical Survey of the Rocky Mountains and spent the next several years exploring this region. When Powell began his work in 1871, he hired E. O. Beaman to make the Survey's photographic record. Beaman resigned in January 1872 and was replaced by James Fennemore of Salt Lake City. Ill health, however, forced Fennemore to leave the Survey and John K. Hillers became the official photographer. Hillers, who subsequently became the chief photographer of the U.S. Geological Survey, was the first to photograph the Grand Canyon, and his photographs of the Indians and geological formations of the Colorado Plateau are now considered classics. Some of Hillers' work, along with that of Beaman, appears here and on the following page. **1** John Wesley Powell and Paiute chief Tau-gu, 1872, by Hillers. **2** High Falls, Bullion Canyon, Utah, by Hillers, 1874. **3** Second Powell Colorado River expedition at Green River Station, Wyoming Territory, May 22, 1871, by Beaman. Powell is the taller of the two men standing in the middle boat. **4** Inner gorge of the Grand Canyon, circa 1872, by Hillers.

1

2

4

3

Photographs from the Powell Survey

5 *Boats in Desolation Canyon, Utah, during Powell's second Colorado River expedition, August 1871, by Beaman.* **6** *Three Patriarchs, Zion Canyon, Utah, 1872, by Hillers.* **7** *Zuni Pueblo, New Mexico, 1879. This is one of a series of photographs made by Hillers while part of a special survey team sent by Powell as director of the Bureau of Ethnology to investigate the archeological ruins and Pueblo Indians of Arizona and New Mexico. Powell's interest in ethnology is reflected in many of Hillers' photographs.*

5

6

7

Armchair Explorations

The literature on the exploration of the American West is vast and one could spend a lifetime reading in it without covering it all. Materials range from the accounts of the explorers themselves, which one should dip into for the sense of wonder and discovery they contain, to recent assessments by modern historians. The books listed below are good secondary accounts, providing details on subjects only lightly dealt with in this booklet. Bibliographies in these works will give additional guidance to those who want to delve even deeper.

Bartlett, Richard A., *Great Surveys of the American West.* University of Oklahoma Press, 1962. Covers the work of the Great Surveys under King, Hayden, Wheeler, and Powell.

Chittenden, Hiram M., *A History of the American Fur Trade of the Far West.* Two volumes. Academic Reprints, 1954. First published in 1902 and still considered the premier work on the subject.

Current, Karen, and William R. Current, *Photography and the Old West.* Abrams, 1978. A perceptive overview, with lots of photographs, of the work of pioneer western photographers, including Jackson, O'Sullivan, and Hillers.

Goetzmann, William H., *Exploration and Empire: The Explorer and the Scientist in the Winning of the American West.* Knopf, 1971. A nearly exhaustive account of western exploration from Lewis and Clark to the Great Surveys.

Hassrick, Peter, *The Way West: Art of Frontier America.* Abrams, 1977. A full pictorial introduction to the work of major artists of the 19th century West, with generous samplings from the works of Catlin, Bodmer, Miller, Bierstadt, Moran, and many others.

Savage, Henry, Jr., *Discovering America, 1700-1875.* Harper and Row, 1979. An informed and highly readable survey, emphasizing the 19th century but including explorations before Lewis and Clark.

Schwartz, Seymour I., and Ralph E. Ehrenberg, *The Mapping of America.* Abrams, 1980. A lavishly illustrated, detailed and analytical history of the mapping of North America from 1500 to the present.

Wilford, John Noble, *The Mapmakers.* Knopf, 1981. The story of the great pioneers in cartography from antiquity to the space age; includes a chapter on the mapping of the trans-Mississippi West.

Index

Abbott, Henry L., 78
Anasazi, 79, 93
Armijo, Antonio, 43
Army, U.S., explorations by, 65-83, 90, 92, 101, 106, 120
Ashley, William H., 28, 35, 44, *45,* 47, 48, 49, 58; expeditions sponsored by, 44-50
Astor John Jacob, 32, *33,* 35, 43
Astorians, 32-35, 44, 46
Audubon, John James, 12, 28, *56,* 57, 100-1; paintings by, *57*
Barlow, John Whitney, 90, 93
Beaman, E. O., 88; photographs by, *123, 124*
Beaver trade, 35, *41,* 49
Beckh, H. V. A., 31
Becknell, William, 39
Beckwith, Edward G., 78
Benton, Thomas Hart, 65, 70, *71*
Bierstadt, Albert, *96-97,* 100, *101,* 102; paintings by, *103*
Bodmer, Karl, 55, 59, 65, 100, *101,* 102; paintings by, *54, 62, 102*
Bonneville, Benjamin L. E., *36-37, 53*
Brewer, William H., 83
Bridger, Jim, 12, *45,* 46, 55
Campbell, Richard, 43
Campbell, Robert, 35, 46
Canyon de Chelly, 79, 93, 101, 120, *121*
Carson, Kit, 55, 70, *72*
Catlin, George, 7, 12, 59, *100,* 102; painting by, *102*
Central Pacific Railroad, 79, 92, 112
Chaco Canyon, 93, 95
Charbonneau, Toissant, 24
Cheyenne Peak, 31
Chouteau, Auguste, 28
Chouteau, Pierre, 28
Clamorgan, Jacques, 39
Clark, William, 12, 21, *24,* 26, 108; map by, *108-09.* See also Lewis and Clark Expedition
Cliff Place (Mesa Verde), *95,* 96
Clyman, James, 45
Colorado River, explorations of, *87,* 88, 90, 92, *111, 120,* 122
Colter, John, 38

"Colter's Hell," 38
Davis, Jefferson, *74,* 78
Death Valley, 83, 92, *120*
Dellenbaugh, Frederick, 88
Doane, Gustavus, 90, 93
Dodge, Grenville M., 78, 112, *113*
Donner Pass, 78, *112*
Drouillard, George, 38, 42
Dunbar, William, 30
Eastman, Seth, 101
Egloffstein, F. W. von, 75, 79, 101
Emory, William H., *74,* 106
Escalante, Padre Sylvestre Valez de, 42, 43
Evans Pass, 78
Europeans, travel and exploration by, 55-65
Fitzpatrick, Tom, 45, 55, 70
Forts: Astoria, 33, 35, 43, *69;* Clark, 55; Clatsop, 26, *27;* Colvile, 50, 70; Fort Union Trading Post, 62; Gibson, 53; Hall, 71; Laramie, *62, 102;* Leavenworth, 74; Manuel's, 38; McKenzie, 59; Nez Perce, 44; Osage, 53; Sutter's, *73;* Union, 56; Vancouver, 50, 63
Frémont, John C., 28, 55, *64,* 79, 106, 110; explorations of, 12, 65, *66-67,* 68, 70-72, *73,* 78
Geological Survey, U.S., 89, 92, 93, 95, 122
Glacier Point (Yosemite), *98,* 99
Glass, Hugh, 45
Grand Canyon of the Colorado, 12, 20, 21, 59, 79, 87, 92, *104-05, 106-07, 120, 122-23*
Gray, Andrew B., 78
"Great American Desert," 15, 19, 31, 32
Great Basin, 20, 44, 47, 50, 71, 72, 79, 80, 89, 90
Great Plains, 15, 19, 20, 30, 31, 51
Great Salt Lake, 42, 44, 50, 72, 78
Great Surveys, The, *82,* 83-95, *114-24.* For individual surveys, see entries under Hayden, King, Powell, and Wheeler
Gunnison, John W., 78, 106

Hayden, Ferdinand V., 80, *92,* 120; surveys of, *82,* 83, *84-85,* 92-93, 101, 107, 110, *116-17, 118-19*
Henry, Andrew, 45
Hill, John Henry, 101
Hillers, John K. ("Jack"), 88, *110;* photographs by, *122-24*
Holmes, William H., 88, 93, *107,* 116; Grand Canyon panorama by, *106-07*
Hudson, William L., 69, 70
Humboldt River, 44
Hunt, Wilson Price, 32-33
Hunter, George, 30
Independence, Mo., 51
Indian tribes: Apache, 20; Arapaho, 20, 39; Arikara, 20, 24, 32, 38, 45, 58; Assiniboin, 58, 59; Bannock, 20; Blackfoot, 20, 58, 59; Chemhuevi, 20; Cheyenne, 20; Comanche, 20, 51; Crow, 20, 45, 46; Flathead, 20; Gosiute, *81;* Gros Ventre, 20; Hopi, 79, 93; Kansa, 20; Kiowa, 20; Mandan, 20, 24, 59, 102; Mohave, 20, 47, 50, 120, *121;* Navajo, 20, 79, 101; Omaha, 20; Osage, 20, 30; Otoe, 20, 58; Paiute, 20, *122;* Papago, 20; Pawnee, 20, 30; Pima, 20; Pueblo, 20, 124; Salish, 33; Sioux, 20, 24, 58; Ute, 20, 78; Yaqui, 20; Yuma, 42
Irving, Washington, 28, 41, 59
Ives, Joseph Christmas, 59, 79, 92, 110
Jackson, David, 45, 50
Jackson, William Henry, 92, 93, 99, *110,* 116, 118; photographs by, *94, 116-19*
Jefferson, Thomas, 8-9, *18,* 19, 21, 24, 25, 30, 32, 35; explorations sponsored or encouraged by, 9, 19-35
Kane, Paul, 101
Kern, Edward, 73
Kern, Richard H., 75, 101
King, Clarence, *80,* 86, 89, *115,* 120; surveys of, 83, *84-85,* 86, 89-90, 93, 101, 107, 110, *114-15*
Langford, Nathaniel P., *90*
Ledyard, John, 9

Lewis, Meriwether, 19, 21, *24, 26*, 30. See also Lewis and Clark Expedition
Lewis and Clark Expedition, 9, 19, 21, *22-23,* 24-26, 28, 30, 33, 35, 38, 45, 58, 83, 106, 107
Lisa, Manuel, 28, *38,* 44, 45, 46
Long, Stephen H., 15, 28, *31,* 106; explorations of, 12, *22-23,* 31-32, 56, 100
Louisiana Purchase, 9, 19, 21, 30, 106
Louisiana Territory, 28, 30, 38, 39
MacKenzie, Alexander, 19
Macomb, John N., 79
Mammoth Hot Springs (Yellowstone), *118*
Maps and mapmakers, 19, 51, 72, 78, 80-81, *106-09*
Mason, Charlie, 95
Maximilien, Alexander Philip, Prince of Wied-Neuwied, 12, *54, 55,* 59, 100
McKenzie, Donald, 33, 43-44
McTavish, John George, 33
Meek, Fielding B., 80, 92
Mesa Verde, 79, *94,* 95, 116, *117*
Michaux, André, 9
Miller, Alfred Jacob, 12, 35, 41, 63, 65, *100;* paintings by, *34, 40, 48-49, 62, 102*
Möllhausen, Heinrich B., 58-59, 75
Montague, Samuel S., 112, *113*
Moran, Thomas, 90, 93, 100, *101, 104, 118;* paintings by, *91, 104-05*
Morse, Jedediah, 19
Moss, John, 116, *117*
Mount of the Holy Cross, 93, *116*
Mountain men, *34,* 35, *40;* explorations by, *36-37,* 38-55
Muybridge, Eadweard, 53, 99, 102; photographs by, *52, 96-97*
Navy, U.S., explorations by, 68-70
Newberry, John S., 12, 79
Nuttall, Thomas, 28, 56, *58, 59*
Ogden, Peter Skene, *44,* 51

"Old Faithful" (Yellowstone), *118*
Old Spanish Trail, 55, 71
Old Spanish Trail (Armijo's), 43
Oregon Trail, 35, 63, 68, 70, 72, 100
O'Sullivan, Timothy, 92, *110, 111,* 114, 120; photographs by, *111, 114-15, 120-21*
Pacific Railroad, surveys for, 58-59, 74-75, *76-77,* 78, 80; construction of, 78-79, *112-13*
Parke, John G., 78, 80
Pattie, James Ohio, 42
Pattie, Sylvester, 42-43
Peale, Titian Ramsay, 100
Photographers, 53, 88, 92, 93, 99, 102, *110-11,* 112, 114, 116, 118, 120, 122, 124
Pike, Zebulon M., 28, *29;* explorations of, 9, *22-23,* 30-31, 32, 39, 106
Pike's Peak, 12, 30, 31
Pope, John B., 78
Powell, John Wesley, 55, *87,* 92, *122, 123,* 124; surveys of, *84-85,* 87-89, 93, 95, 101, 104, 107, 110, *122-24*
Prescott, Ariz., 55
Promontory, Utah, 79, 112
Provost, Etienne, 42, 46
Raynolds, William F., 80
Rendezvous system, 41, 46-47, *48-49,* 50, 53, 63, 65
"Rio Buenaventura" (mythical), search for, 20, 32, 47, 50, 71
Robinson, Sanford, 101
Ross, Alexander, 46
Russell, Andrew J., 112
Ruxton, Frederick, 41, 59
Sacagawea, 26, 58
St. Louis, 26, *28-29*
Salt Lake City, 88, 114, *115*
Salt Lake Desert, *81*
Sante Fe, 20, 39
Santa Fe Trail, 39
Seymour, Samuel, 31, 100
Shoshone Falls, 114, *115*
Silliman, Benjamin, 86-87
Simpson, James Hervey, 79, *80,* 81, 106, 110
Sitgreaves, Lorenzo, 79
Smith, Jedediah, 12, 44, *47,* 89; travels of, *36-37,* 43, 45-47, 50-51

Sohon, Gustave, 75, 101
South Pass, 35, 38, 46, 51, 53, 65, 68, 71
Sparks, Thomas, 30
Stanley, John Mix, 75, 101
Stansbury, Howard, 78, 101
Stephens, Isaac I., 74-75, 78, 110
Stewart, Sir William Drummond, 12, 59, 62-65, 70
Stuart, Robert, 35
Sublette, William, 28, 35, 45, 50, 63
Umpqua "massacre," 50
Union Pacific Railroad, *78,* 79, 112
Union Pass, 33, 46
Walker, Joseph Reddeford, *53;* explorations by, *36-37,* 51-55, 71
Walker Pass, 53
Warren, Gouverneur K., 107; master map of the West by, 80-81, 108, *109*
Washburn, Henry D., *90*
Wetherill, Richard, 95
Wheeler, George M., surveys of, *84-85,* 90, *92,* 93, 101, 107, 110, *111, 120-21*
Whipple, Amiel Weeks, 58-59, 78, 106
Whitney, Joseph D., 83, 86, 87, 89
Wilhelm, Frederick Paul, Duke of Württemberg, travels of, 56, 58, 60; Western collection of, 58, *60-61*
Wilkes, Charles, naval expedition of, *66-67,* 68-70, 71
Williams, Bill, 78
Wyeth, Nathaniel, 56, 63
Yellowstone National Park, 38, 51, *91;* exploration and establishment of, 90, 92-93, 116, *118-19*
Yellowstone region, 12, 63, 110
Yosemite, 12, 83, 86, 93, *96-97, 98,* 99, 102, 103
Young, John J., 81, 101
Zion Canyon, 88, *124*

For sale by the Superintendent of Documents, U.S. Government Printing Office, Washington, DC 20402. Stock Number 024-005-00834-9.

☆ GPO: 1982—361-611/102.

The National Park Service expresses its appreciation to all those persons who made the preparation and production of this handbook possible. The Service also gratefully acknowledges the financial support given this handbook project by the Jefferson National Expansion Memorial Association, a nonprofit group that assists interpretive efforts at Jefferson National Expansion Memorial.

Texts
Richard A. Bartlett, who wrote about the "Lure of the West" in Part 1, is professor of American history at Florida State University, Tallahassee, and has written extensively on the westward movement.

William H. Goetzmann, author of "Explorer, Mountain Man, and Scientist" in Part 2, is a professor of history at the University of Texas at Austin, where he also heads the American Studies Program. His books include *Army Exploration in the American West, 1803-1863,* and *Exploration and Empire: The Explorer and Scientist in the Winning of the American West.*

Illustrations
The Bancroft Library, University of California, Berkeley, 73; Henry B. Beville, 103; Buffalo Bill Historical Center, Cody, Wyoming, 40, 41 (pistol); University of California, Berkeley, 115 (top, right); University of California, Los Angeles, 52; California Historical Society Library, 96-97; Colorado Historical Society, 90 (Langford), 94; Culver Pictures, Inc., 64; Denver Public Library, 53 (Bonneville), 98; R. R. Donnelley Cartographic Service, 22-23, 36-37, 66-67, 76-77, 84-85; Dick Dorrance, 27; East Hampton Free Library, 101 (Moran); Gilcrease Institute of History & Art, 100 (Miller); Henry E. Huntington Library and Art Gallery, 112 (top); Independence National Historical Park, 24, 30, 31; International Museum of Photography, George Eastman House, Rochester, N.Y., 110 (O'Sullivan), 111 (Camera and accessories), 121 (bottom); Joslyn Art Museum, Omaha, cover, 53 (Walker), 62 (center), 102 (center & bottom); The Kansas State Historical Society, Topeka, 45 (Bridger), 47; Kit Carson Memorial Foundation, New Mexico, 72; Russell Lamb, 10-11; Library of Congress, 57, 58, 59, 68, 74, 75, 80, 101 (Bodmer), 107 (Holmes), 108 (bottom), 110 (Hillers), 115 (top, left, & bottom), 117 (top), 118 (top), 120 (bottom), 121 (top, right), 124 (bottom); Missouri Historical Society, St. Louis, 25, 38, 41 (beaver hat), 45 (newspaper ad); David Meunch, 4-5, 6, 13, 14; Museum of the Fur Trade, Chadron, Neb., 41 (beaver trap); National Archives, 81, 82, 92(Wheeler), 109 (Warren & Wheeler maps), 110 (Jackson), 111 (stereograph), 114, 116 (top), 118 (bottom), 119 (bottom), 120 (top), 121 (top, left), 122-23, 124 (top & center); National Collection of Fine Arts, Smithsonian Institution, 91; National Museum of American Art, Smithsonian Institution, 102 (top), 104-5; National Park Service, 21, 87; National Portrait Gallery, Smithsonian Institution, 33, 100 (Catlin); New York Public Library, 54, 69; North Dakota Tourism Promotion, Bismarck, 26; Oregon Historical Society, 44; Peregrine Smith Books, Layton, Utah, 106-7 (Holmes panorama); Public Archives of Canada, 62 (top); St. Louis Art Museum, 16-17, 28-29; Staatliches Museum für Naturkunde, Stuttgart, Germany, 60-61; U.S. Geological Survey, 89, 92 (Hayden); Union Pacific Railroad Museum Collections, 78, 113 (top); Walker Art Gallery, Liverpool, England, 56; Walters Art Gallery, Baltimore, 34, 62 (bottom); The Whaling Museum, New Bedford, 101 (Bierstadt); The White House, 18; University of Wyoming, American Heritage Center, 48-49; Yale University Library, 108-9 (Clark map), 112 (bottom), 113 (bottom).